WALKING THE GLOUCESTERSHIRE WAY

ONE-WEEK HIKE FROM CHEPSTOW TO TEWKESBURY

by Daniel Hughes

CICERONE

JUNIPER HOUSE, MURLEY MOSS,
OXENHOLME ROAD, KENDAL, CUMBRIA LA9 7RL
cicerone.co.uk

First edition 2026
ISBN: 978 1 78631 294 5
eISBN: 978 1 78765 266 8

Printed in China on responsibly sourced paper on behalf of Latitude Press Ltd.
A catalogue record for this book is available from the British Library.
All photographs are by the author unless otherwise stated.

Cicerone's EU representative for GPSR compliance is Easy Access System Europe, Mustamäe tee 50, 10621 Tallinn, Estonia. Email gpsr.requests@easproject.com.

Dedication

Gerry Stewart developed and championed this walk over 30 years. He was a tireless campaigner for greater access to the countryside and an enthusiast for Gloucestershire and its treasures. He was the author of the original guidebook and the debt to him is immense. He remains greatly missed.

Updates to this guide

While we strive to ensure that our guidebooks are as up to date and accurate as possible, changes can occur during the lifetime of an edition. Facilities, accommodation, transport and even rights of way can change, so if you find any inaccuracies in this book or have any feedback please let us know by email at updates@cicerone.co.uk. Updates will be published on the Cicerone website (cicerone.co.uk/1294/updates), so please check before planning your trip.

To receive free updates, special offers and GPX files where available, don't forget to register your book at the 'My Account' tab at cicerone.co.uk.

Front cover: Barley field before Upper Coberley (Stage 5)

CONTENTS

Route symbols on OS map extracts
(for OS legend see printed OS maps)

- route
- alternative route
- link route/detour
- SF start/finish point
- S start point
- F finish point
- route direction

SCALE: 1:50,000

0 kilometres 0.5 1
0 miles 0.5

Features on the overview map

- county/unitary boundary
- national boundary
- urban area
- forest park/national forest eg ***National Forest***
- national landscapes eg *The Cotswolds*

400m
200m
75m
0m

GPX files for all routes can be downloaded free at cicerone.co.uk/1294/GPX.

Acknowledgements

This book draws on Gerry's original guide: thanks to him and his family for permission to do this. The Eleven Rivers group, established to promote this and other long-distance walks, has provided helpful critique and assistance. Cotswold Voluntary Wardens have helped with signage and advice in that part of the way. Gloucestershire County Council Public Rights of Way team has been supportive and has responded only with helpfulness to my many reports of issues on the route. Gloucestershire Geology Trust cast an eye over that section of the book (faults remaining are mine, however). Thank you to Gloucestershire Cathedral for their permission to publish the photo of the Gurney Window and to The Ivor Gurney Estate for the poem *East Wind* in Stage 4.

ROUTE SUMMARY TABLE

Stage	Start	Finish	Time	Distance	Ascent	Descent	Page
1	Chepstow	Parkend	5hr 30mins	19.1km	430m	305m	28
2	Parkend	Boxbush	5hr 25mins	18.8km	420m	410m	38
3	Boxbush	Gloucester	5hr 35mins	20.5km	250m	325m	48
4	Gloucester	Shurdington	4hr 20mins	16.5km	90m	8m	58
5	Shurdington	Shipton Oliffe	4hr 40mins	15.6km	440m	330m	66
6	Shipton Oliffe	Stow-on-the-Wold	6hr 10mins	21.9km	340m	280m	74
7	Stow-on-the-Wold	Winchcombe	6hr	21.7km	300m	445m	84
8	Winchcombe	Tewkesbury	5hr 5mins	18.2km	265m	345m	93

Donnington Brewery (Stage 7)

ROUTE PROFILE

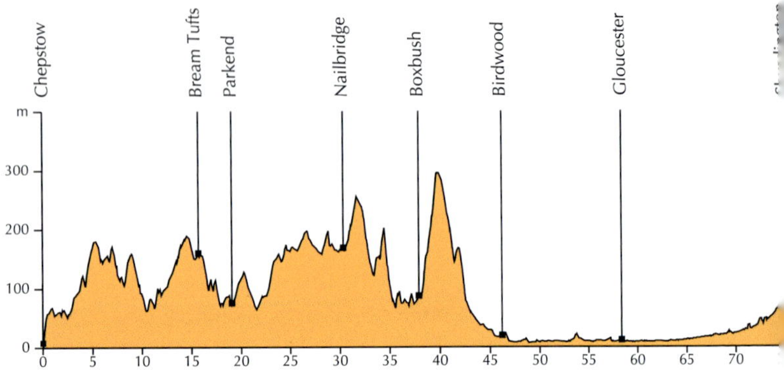

8 DAYS				
	Chepstow to Parkend *5hr 30min* *19.1km*	Parkend to Boxbush *5hr 25min* *18.8km*	Boxbush to Gloucester *5hr 35min* *20.5km*	Gloucester to Shurdington *4hr 20min* *16.5km*

5 DAYS			
	Chepstow to Nailbridge *8hr 40min* *30.3km*	Nailbridge to Gloucester *7hr 50min* *28.1km*	Gloucester to Shipton Oli *9hr* *32.1km*

10 DAYS					
	Chepstow to Bream Tufts *4hr 35min* *15.7km*	Bream Tufts to Nailbridge *4hr 5min* *14.6km*	Nailbridge to Birdwood *4hr 45min* *15.9km*	Birdwood to Gloucester *3hr 5min* *12.2km*	Gloucester to Shurdington *4hr 20min* *16.5km*

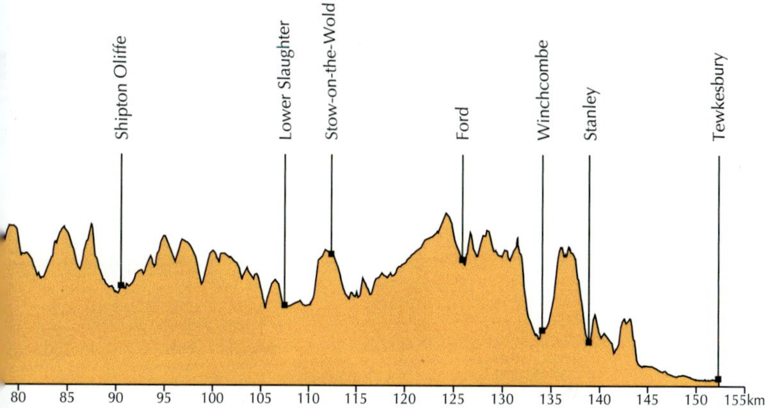

hurdington to hipton Oliffe *4hr 40min* *15.6km*	Shipton Oliffe to Stow-on-the-Wold *6hr 10min* *21.9km*	Stow-on-the-Wold to Winchcombe *6hr* *21.7km*	Winchcombe to Tewkesbury *5hr 5min* *18.2km*

AVERAGE DAY – 19km / 5hr 20min

	Shipton Oliffe to Ford *9hr 50min* *35.4km*	Ford to Tewkesbury *7hr 25min* *26.4km*

AVERAGE DAY – 30.5km / 8hr 33min

Shurdington o Shipton Oliffe *4hr 40min* *15.6km*	Shipton Oliffe to Lower Slaughter *4hr 50min* *17.3km*	Lower Slaughter to Ford *5hr* *18.1km*	Ford to Stanley *3hr 50min* *13km*	Stanley to Tewkesbury *3hr 35min* *13.4km*

AVERAGE DAY – 15.2km / 4hr 16min

Cross at Condicote (Stage 7)

INTRODUCTION

Enjoying the contours of Coldwell Bottom (Stage 5)

The Gloucestershire Way (GW) showcases the distinctive scenery of the county, passing through the Forest of Dean, the Severn Vale and the Cotswolds. It takes as its theme a line from a poem by FW Harvey (the 'poet laureate of Gloucestershire'): "Forest and vale and high blue hill".

In sight of the oldest stone castle in these islands, the Gloucestershire Way starts at the ancient Wales-England border, on the old Wye Bridge in Chepstow. It rises through gentle hills to gain majestic views of Britain's longest and largest river, the Severn, in its serpentine coilings before meeting the Atlantic.

The GW then passes into the Forest of Dean, an ancient woodland, but one that has supported extraction industries from Neolithic times. Within the forest are old mine and quarry workings, and where now there are quiet villages, there were once busy foundries and forges. Former railways and tramlines have been repurposed as leisure paths into the tranquil woods, but the evidence of the industrial past is all around, in the form of station signs, tracks, mill reservoirs, old chimneys and workings. Thus, peace and beauty abide by a rich industrial heritage. There is evidence of efforts at management and conservation of the woodlands that began centuries ago. Partly this was to preserve royal hunting grounds, but the need to replenish timber taken for shipbuilding or charcoal-making was also a stimulus to tree-planting and enclosure.

Lower Slaughter (Stage 6)

Walkers emerge from the forest to climb May Hill, which has panoramic views including far into Wales, north to Herefordshire, and east to where the journey heads: the great Cotswold escarpment. From here the route is downhill to the River Severn, along its banks and through its vale to the ancient city of Gloucester, which boasts one of the finest cathedrals in the world. You should pause here to take in the sights and then continue across the vale through quiet lanes and farmlands, towards the looming Cotswold Hills, always in sight ahead.

The GW crosses the Cotswold Way high up on Crickley Hill, which overlooks the Severn Vale, which from here can seem as flat as a billiard table and stretches far into the misty distance. But unlike the wonderful Cotswold Way, which holds to the escarpment edge, this walk heads into the Cotswolds, visiting innumerable honey-coloured villages and taking in the big skies and great space of these gorgeous rolling hills. Walkers can choose to visit tiny churches, many dating back 800 or more years, and lunch in old hostelries, formerly waypoints for journeys east to Oxford and London. The Cotswolds is a region of living and working countryside, but is an Area of Outstanding Natural Beauty (AONB), and its old drystone walls and ancient field systems are conserved for now and future enjoyment.

At the pretty market town of Stow-on-the-Wold, the route turns and heads back westwards passing through a more empty and open landscape before reaching another lovely old town, Winchcombe, where the Cotswold Way is crossed once more. From here, the final hills again provide views westwards across the Severn, towards Bristol, the Midlands, Malverns and Wales. The Gloucestershire Way then recrosses the Severn Vale, to complete the journey at the historic medieval town of Tewkesbury, with its fine abbey, another ecclesiastical gem.

A BRIEF HISTORY OF THE GLOUCESTERSHIRE WAY

In 1990, Gloucester took its turn to host the Three Choirs Festival. Local groups, the Tewkesbury Walking Club and Cleeve Ramblers, determined to develop some walks as part of the events and decided to base these loosely on the poetry of local writers. A route was identified, and stalwarts set off on a series of expeditions to 'test-walk' the suggested way. Over the following years, Gerry Stewart (roping in particularly his immediate family members) pursued this project with verve and tenacity. Gerry was in the happy position of being both in the Public Rights of Way team at Gloucestershire County Council and a leading light among local ramblers. By 1996 a definitive route had been agreed, and the first edition of Gerry's guidebook was published.

The route was actively supported by Gloucestershire County Council, and in 2000 a grant from the Millennium Fund was secured that allowed improved access to be developed at various points, and that notably paid for the high-quality cast-iron signage that remains in place today (with only a few casualties to hedge cutters). Just by the red railway arches, coming into Gloucester, there is an ornate kissing gate, which commemorates the opening of the way, and its association with Millennium celebrations.

Gerry Stewart continued to be the foremost champion of the Gloucestershire Way, undertaking significant revisions of his guidebook in 2002, 2007 and 2018, which he self-published and promoted. The books are brought to life with exquisite line drawings by Genny Proctor.

With advancing years, Gerry sought to find new blood to sustain the Gloucestershire Way and, in 2022, a group – Eleven Rivers – was formed to take on the promotion and maintenance of this and other local long-distance paths. Although the way largely still follows the route devised in the 1990s, it has always evolved and adapted to changes, such as new housing or the changing course of footpaths. The large road-building project underway around the A417 will much improve the route (and safety) of this and the Cotswold Way. Similarly, although Gerry's self-published book remains a great guide, it

Cotswold fossils

is hoped that this Cicerone book will reach a wider audience and so introduce this wonderful journey to a new generation of walkers.

GLOUCESTERSHIRE

Gloucestershire is a largely rural county sitting towards the south-west of England and bordering Wales. Its highest point, on Cleeve Hill at the edge of the Cotswolds, is some 330m, but overall it can be considered a low-lying area with no part difficult to access either on foot or by vehicle. Its terrain is not hazardous or challenging, and although this way will be delightful to all, it might be considered well-suited to novices of long-distance walking or those who prefer their expeditions a little less demanding.

The main urban centres of the county are in its centre at Gloucester and Cheltenham, which are only 15km apart and enjoy excellent transport links. There are significantly sized towns at Stroud, Tewkesbury and Cirencester, with smaller towns distributed through the district along with innumerable villages. With the mass ownership of cars, and the movement of employment away from agriculture, many of the smaller villages are without amenities such as shops or inns. Walkers should not hope for such establishments where none are marked or mentioned in the text.

The theme of the walk – "Forest and vale and high blue hill" – well reflects the actual division of the county into distinct geographical areas, which in turn have varying histories. There is evidence of prehistoric human impact throughout the county, perhaps best seen on this walk on Crickley Hill at the start of the Cotswolds, where excavations have evidenced habitation from 5500 years ago, seemingly punctuated by regular violence. Neolithic groups flourished here for centuries, before abandoning the location, possibly after some great battle. Undoubtedly attracted by its strategic location with defensible hillsides and commanding views, Iron Age tribes subsequently settled here too and again there is evidence that it was violently attacked, stoutly defended and then abandoned.

Much of the time, walkers are following in the footsteps of countless generations, stretching back into prehistory. The Salt Way, crossed twice (near Salperton and again above Winchcombe), which runs from Droitwich to Lechlade, is named for the medieval trade in salt. But it is certain those merchants and hauliers were using routes developed before Roman times. Likewise, the route following the escarpment, now repurposed in places as the Cotswold Way, would have been a major highway for prehistoric peoples. The limestone feature, that runs from the Humber in the north to Dorset in the south, is higher than surrounding lands, so drier and more easily navigated.

The Romans came to Gloucestershire and there are ruins of villas noted throughout the Cotswolds. But their biggest settlements were on the Severn at Gloucester – Glevum; and at Cirencester – Corinium. The Museum of Gloucester gives an account of their stay in that city. Several important Roman roads run through the area, including the Ermin Way from Cirencester to Gloucester (now largely replaced by the A417) and the Fosseway, which ran from Exeter to Lincoln, and passed through Corinium and is met on this walk at

Chepstow Castle (Stage 1)

Stow-on-the-Wold (and is also repurposed as a major A road).

It was with the Normans that the shape of the county started to become settled. Gloucester was immediately adopted as a place of strategic importance, and it was here that William commissioned the Doomsday Book. The greatest legacy of the Normans is undoubtedly Gloucester Cathedral, but many other churches encountered on the walk have elements dating from this time. Nearly all churches passed are open and accessible, and most will have some observations within on their history and heritage.

The Cotswolds were shaped notably by the wool trade in the Middle Ages. This created enormous wealth, which is reflected in the fine manor houses and churches that can still be seen today. Walkers are certain to encounter the Cotswold Lion – a breed of sheep perfectly suited to these hills, which produces a heavy thick fleece. The landscape is criss-crossed by iconic drystone walls (Cotswolds means pens on the hill-side), which hold the sheep in their fields. Daniel Dafoe observed in the 1720s that 20,000 sheep might pass through Stow market in a single day – a lay estimate that has acquired the status of fact over the centuries. The Cotswolds remain gentle countryside dotted with towns, villages and hamlets, many stunningly beautiful.

The history of the Forest of Dean includes a tension between a desire to preserve and enhance the woodland, both for timber and as a hunting park; and efforts to exploit the mineral riches of the area, in particular coal and iron. The industry has now nearly all gone, but its remnants are everywhere in the form of old railways, ruins of foundry works, repurposed track and so on. It takes only a little imagination to picture a past world of noise and fire in what are now the tranquil glades of the forest. Many of the plantations date back several centuries, reflecting the concern to secure supplies of timber, particularly for shipbuilding. The different trees encountered through the forest result as much from decisions about planting as from any natural processes. With the demise of industry, the extent of forest now is greater than it has been in the recent past, and there is an abundance of wildlife, including a healthy population of wild boar whose reintroduction was by stealth or accident.

The central Severn Vale has long been used as a highway both by the river and by land and this continues today. It is said that putting a spade in the ground in Gloucester means going through several layers of history and there is plenty to see there, including its museums and medieval buildings. Cheltenham is a newer town, having its heyday as a Georgian spa in the late 18th century. It remains a pleasant good-sized town, with festivals throughout the year, the biggest being the spring horse-racing meeting, always held near St Patrick's day

View of Hay Bluff from May Hill summit (Stage 3)

– 17 March – and considered the most prestigious jump meet in the country. (It is still possible to taste Cheltenham's spa water, although this is not recommended by this author!)

GEOLOGY

Unsurprisingly, the differences in the observable landscape of the county of Gloucestershire arise from the distinctive geology of the three main areas.

The Forest of Dean sits on a bed of Old Red Sandstone which reaches the surface at its edges near the Severn and Wye rivers and also emerges from the forest towards May Hill at the north. Fields here can take on a deep red tinge when fallow. Some of the old stone-built cottages share this bright colour as does Telford's Bridge, at Over. Overlying the sandstone is carboniferous limestone, which is ore-bearing and also reaches the surface in areas to the east, north and particularly western sides of the forest. On top of this limestone are Coal Measures, which cover most of the area of the forest. Much of this is coal bearing and, unusually, most of the coal is near the surface. Thus, cottage industries of coal mining preceded the deeper mines of the 19th and 20th century and, to a small extent, continue today.

May Hill, incidentally, is an outlier of older Silurian rocks: a mixture of limestone, shale and sandstone rocks (the latter fostering the short-lived glass industry on its flanks).

The Severn Vale is composed predominantly of mudstone, which is not much use as a building material. This required the development of brick-making, which particularly occurred under the Cotswold scarp, utilizing Lias clays laid down there. These clays, unfortunately for the brick-makers (fortuitously for everyone else), contain numerous marine fossils which tend to explode during firing and so needed to be crushed or removed. The brickworks that clustered in Cheltenham at the end of the 19th century attracted fossil-hunters happy to exploit the diggings.

The Cotswolds are characteristically Jurassic Oolitic Limestone, laid down in warm seas about 160 million years ago. The rocks are often rich in fossils of sea-creatures, and it's worth keeping an eye open for these when crossing fields. This band of limestone stretches from the southern English coast to the Humber estuary. The prominent high ground provided early humans with an easier route for walking cross country, so that the line followed by today's paths and roads (north-east to south-west) is actually retracing ways forged in Neolithic times. The shading of the limestone varies depending on its content of other minerals (so old houses in Stow-on-the-Wold and Winchcombe have a slightly different tint). Fresh from the quarry, the stone has a rich syrupy colour, but this will usually fade with weathering to the lighter greys seen in the houses and walls passed. The stone remains highly prized for house building. Limestone is free-draining and easily farmed, hence the presence of agriculture here for millennia past and into the future. (Limestone is also great for walkers, tending not to get boggy or muddy.)

Pony in the Forest of Dean (Stage 2)

CONSERVATION STATUS

The Forest of Dean, in 1938, was the first designated National Forest in England, although it has enjoyed protection and royal status since Saxon times. It is now managed by Forestry England and continues to be commercially exploited, these days mainly for timber and building stone. However, this is combined and balanced with conservation efforts and in early 2025 the local authority began the process of becoming a UNESCO Biosphere. Explicit within the application is the need to integrate conservation, commercial exploitation, tourism and cultural heritage. The range of habitats, including forest and heath, provide a stronghold for innumerable species of animal; for example, it hosts the largest colonies of greater and lesser horseshoe bats in Europe. Much of the forest is free from day-to-day human exploitation, and so provides a refuge for many animals, including large mammals, such as ponies, deer and boar.

The Cotswolds was designated an Area of Outstanding Natural Beauty (AONB) in 1966, with the boundaries extended in 1990. It is the largest such area in England, incorporating parts of several counties, and extending nearly 150km from Stratford to Bath. The legal designation of AONB remains, however, the 46 such areas have rebranded themselves as National Landscapes, to create a consistency of style and to stress their importance to national life and well-being. The Cotswolds is very much a working area with most of the land devoted to mixed agriculture. Although past wealth was associated with sheep farming, and this continues today, other livestock also thrive here, and walkers will pass fields of wheat, barley and other crops. In late spring, don't miss the fields resplendent with oil seed rape, a crop that has massively increased in recent decades. There are multiple wildlife habitats within the Cotswolds, but possibly the most iconic are the limestone grasslands and meadows which historically supported a rich diversity of plants and insects. These areas suffered and diminished with the intensification of agriculture from the early 20th century onwards, but throughout the area there are now successful efforts at restoration. Pay attention to field boundaries and smaller areas set aside for nature.

PLANNING THE WALK

When to go?

The Gloucestershire Way can be undertaken in any season although account will need to be taken of the expected weather day-to-day. All seasons contain their delights, but spring and autumn are particularly lovely with, respectively, the abundance of early flowers and the changing colours of foliage. As with anywhere in Britain, it is impossible to predict the weather far in advance: there can be lovely sunny days in winter; and grisly rain in

The Gloucestershire Way can be walked in both directions (Stage 5)

high summer. That said, summer will be warmer and tends also to be drier.

Walkers will never be far from a road or from human habitation. If extreme conditions unexpectedly arise, shelter can be found.

Winter rain will inevitably lead to wetter conditions underfoot, and there will be muddy sections. However, most of the walk is over well-drained ground, so this is not a persistent problem. The Cotswolds usually become very dry in summer.

Which direction?

In Britain, walking lore has it that heading north or east keeps the elements more at your back than when walking south or west. For the Gloucestershire Way, this is a minor consideration. The step-by-step instructions below are given south to north, starting in Chepstow and ending in Tewkesbury, but the guide with points of interest, advice and route map can be used in either direction. Both ends are easily accessed by public transport.

How long will it take?

Although the Gloucestershire Way could be extended over two weeks, most walkers will want to proceed at a faster clip. See the Route Profile on page 6 for suggested itineraries for 5, 8 and 10 days' walking .

Stage planning

This guide has broken the journey into eight stages of roughly 15–20km, and each stage has been subdivided into shorter sections that will take up to two hours to complete. In practice few walkers will want to stick exactly to the itinerary of stages. There are limited accommodation opportunities along the route, and finding a roof for the night is likely to be the significant factor in determining each day's extent.

The timings for stages and subsections are calculated using a variant of

Naismith's rule, in this case that it will take 15 minutes to walk a kilometre with an allowance of an additional minute for every 10m of height gain. Walkers will quickly learn if this over- or underestimates their speed. There are no other significant impediments to progress (eg difficult terrain, navigational challenges, etc).

Many will use this guide as inspiration for shorter day walks, either with a return by public transport to the start or finding an alternative way back, thereby creating a circular day-walk. Although many folk these days will have GPS devices or mapping applications on their phones, the required paper maps from the OS 1:25,000 series are included in each stage introduction. Across the entire walk only four are needed:

- OL14: Wye Valley & Forest of Dean
- Explorer 179: Gloucester, Cheltenham & Stroud
- OL45: The Cotswolds
- Explorer 190: Malvern Hills & Bredon Hill

These allow a greater extent of terrain to be surveyed and variants devised.

Breaks and stopping points

Points of interest have been noted in the text, and a good rule-of-thumb is that any church passed will be open and worth a quick visit. Gloucester Cathedral and Tewkesbury Abbey are outstanding monuments of global significance. The towns of Chepstow, Gloucester, Stow, Winchcombe and Tewkesbury visited on the walk are well worth the delay. Cheltenham too is an easy diversion and will repay a visit or a night's stay. Bourton-on-the-Water is extremely picturesque, but often very crowded.

Options for refreshment have been included in the text and stage information boxes. Others will be available but will require greater diversion from the route. As elsewhere in Britain, many public houses have closed in recent years and, as a result, there are sections where there are longer gaps between hostelries. If your walk is reliant on a particular shop, pub or inn being open, always check ahead to make sure it will be ready to greet you when you get there.

Accommodation

When planning the walk, accommodation must be booked in advance. Appendix A includes some accommodation listings, but often walkers will be better served reviewing the tourism websites, which have been included in Appendix B. Consideration should be given to staying in the same accommodation for more than one night, and using public transport or taxis between there and the stage end/start. In the more touristy parts of the Cotswolds it can be difficult to find lodgings for a single night. Longer-stay self-catering or the likes of Airbnb may also be options, particularly if you have the benefit of a 'support-team' ready to ferry you to and from the route.

Wild camping is not allowed anywhere along the route. While it might be possible to find a secluded spot in the Forest of Dean, elsewhere the route is through farmland, and wild campers are unlikely to be welcomed. Campsites do exist along the Gloucestershire Way, although not at a frequency or regularity that negates a need to plan. Some deviation from the route will be unavoidable.

Sadly, there are no hostels along the way, although YHA St Briavels is about 4km off route and ,for some, staying in an 800-year-old castle may be a temptation too great to miss.

Most accommodation will be available throughout the year, and any closure in winter is likely to be matched by reduced demand. Some of the Cheltenham festivals can impact the availability and price of accommodation to the east of the Severn, and the spring horse-racing meeting (mid-March) is probably worth avoiding (unless you want to fit in a day at the races!).

Variants, onward journeys and shorter routes

This is a low-level walk in English countryside that is riddled with public rights of way and quiet lanes. As a result, there are any number of variants that could be devised for purposes as diverse as finding a cup of tea or visiting a particular church. The only two variants discussed in detail in the text are: an alternative route out of the Forest of Dean

The Mill, Lower Slaughter (Stage 6)

GWR steaming at Gotherington Halt (Stage 8)

to May Hill, which visits the small town of Mitcheldean and uses the line of the Wysis Way; and an alternative to the Severnside route out of Gloucester, which goes along city roads instead.

For those with time and energy, numerous other long-distance paths cross the Gloucestershire Way and could be combined to form even longer routes. These are pointed out in the text. Picking up the Cotswold Way in Winchcombe (or, better, devising a route to Cleeve Hill from Oxenton) and walking south towards Bath will extend time in Gloucestershire and visit the glorious beechwoods further along the escarpment.

It is easy to start or finish the Gloucestershire Way at any point along its route, to fit the journey into whatever time is available. Walkers with limited time might also consider taking public transport from Huntley (just after May Hill) to Shurdington (just before the climb into the Cotswolds), saving the best part of two days' walking. This involves bypassing Gloucester Cathedral (although the change of bus or an overnight stop in Gloucester could be combined with a visit). This is not to denigrate the journey across the Severn Vale, but walkers may decide what restricted time they have is best spent in the Forest of Dean and then the Cotswolds.

Transport options

There are mainline train stations at Chepstow, Lydney, Gloucester, Cheltenham and Ashchurch (for Tewkesbury). Trains are frequent enough between these stations to make them a viable option for progressing along the route. There is a station at Moreton-in-Marsh (on the Oxford to Worcester line), but this is likely only to be useful as a means of arriving at or leaving Stow from elsewhere in the country.

Huge skies around Condicote (Stage 7)

Main bus routes have been listed in Appendix B. Buses tend to run from smaller towns towards Gloucester or Cheltenham; they are usually regular and continue into the early evening. But you should always check before the start of the day, and plan for exigencies. Traveline is a good application to have on your phone. Stagecoach is the biggest operator, with two Cotswold routes being provided by Pulhams.

Taxis or Ubers can be summoned to just about any road crossing the route, so it may be wise to identify local companies before setting off.

As noted above, an option may be to stay several nights in one location and then take public transport or taxis to and from the route each day.

There are two heritage railways along the route. The Dean Forest Railway runs between Lydney and Parkend, while the Gloucestershire Warwickshire Steam Railway runs from Cheltenham Racecourse (some way from the Cheltenham Spa station) to Broadway, via Gotherington and Winchcombe.

EQUIPMENT AND PRACTICALITIES

No special equipment is needed for this walk. Footwear needs to be comfortable and suitable for walking long days in rough terrain. In wet conditions you should either have waterproof boots or be tolerant of wet feet! Clothing needs to be suitable for the weather expected. Being England, you should be really – REALLY – confident of no rain before setting out without waterproofs. Be aware that footpaths can be narrow and, in summer, very overgrown, so either be ready to tolerate a few stings and scratches, or else wear long trousers. Covering arms and legs also deters ticks.

The Gloucestershire Way is reasonably well waymarked, particularly from roads into footpaths. But this is not a route where a flash or sign is always visible. Walkers will need additional guidance either from the route description or a map and ideally both. If planning to rely on a phone application, it is wise to download maps before setting off, and uploading the GPX file provided. It is also sensible to carry power boosters, as navigation can quickly drain your battery. It is usually better to neither "follow" nor "create" a route with your phone: these are power-hungry. Keeping your phone in "flight mode" is another way of reducing power demand. Applications specifically intended for off-road walking should be used (such as the Cicerone app, OS Maps, OutdoorActive, Organic Maps, etc). GoogleMaps or AppleMaps are not intended for walking navigation, although will be useful for other purposes, such as finding shops or accommodation. Having a physical paper map (contained in a waterproof wallet) is always a good idea.

A mobile phone signal is generally present throughout this walk.

Mains water that comes out of a tap at pressure is drinkable. Anything else should be avoided (or treated). Be sure to carry enough water to get you to the next settlement, and drink regularly.

A first-aid kit should include a few small plasters for minor cuts. It's sensible to carry antihistamine tablets to counter allergies. Although it is unusual to spot ticks attached to you while walking, a device to remove them is handy. Sunshine that causes your skin to change colour has harmed you. Protect yourself with sunglasses, a hat, clothing and sun cream.

This guide prefers to use instructions such as left, right, straight ahead. However, in forested areas, where finding points of orientation is difficult, the guide does use compass points also. So, carrying a compass or having such an application on your phone is likely to be helpful.

ON THE GLOUCESTERSHIRE WAY

The terrain

The Gloucestershire Way is entirely on existing roads, public rights of way and, in parts of the Forest of Dean, on Access Land with well-established customary access. For the most part, the paths can easily be identified on the ground. Where the path is clear, please stick to it. Most rights of way are over private property, and the existence of a path does not betoken the right of access to adjoining land.

Mostly paths are well drained and are easy to use in any season.

Sign at Lower Slaughter – all roads lead to Stow! (Stage 6)

A few can become muddy in winter, dusty in summer. They are also prone to overgrowth in summer, which is sometimes scratchy and stingy. Paths across fields cannot be diverted unless by agreement and order. Where ploughing and planting have occurred, the path should be reinstated shortly after. This said, be pragmatic, and if a short detour around a field boundary avoids damaging crops, then do take it.

Despite the best efforts of Gerry Stewart, a tireless campaigner for improved countryside access, there are countless stiles along this route. Walkers will need to be able to clamber over these. At no other time are hands needed to make progress over the terrain.

Human hazards

The greatest hazard the walker will face on the Gloucestershire Way is road traffic. Road walking is kept to a minimum and any extended sections of road are on quiet country lanes. All road crossing and road walking requires vigilance and full attention. Children should be closely supervised. Earphones should be removed so that hearing is as good as it can be.

There are three rail crossings along the route, all with excellent sight lines and just two tracks. In all cases the rule is, if you can see or hear a train don't cross. This includes allowing trains just passed to travel a significant distance so that you can be certain no train is coming from the other direction.

Occasionally gunfire may be heard; this is usually clay-pigeon, grouse or pheasant shooting. Such activities should never create a hazard for walkers who are sticking to public rights of way. If shooting is heard, confirm for yourself that it is not on the path you are following and carry on.

Animal hazards

Farmers should not be creating hazards on fields crossed by footpaths. Walkers may well encounter cattle, and the general rule is to keep dogs on a short lead and to avoid coming between a cow and her calf. Most cows are curious but untroubled by walkers. Dogs are involved in most adverse incidents with cattle and the guidance is that if a cow becomes distressed or aggressive, release the dog and get yourself to safety.

Ticks are present throughout the countryside in the UK. They clamber up vegetation and transfer to a host animal when it (or you) brushes past. The tick will often move from an extremity towards a more fleshy part of the body (eg higher up the arm, or the midriff). Ticks may carry Lyme disease which can pass to a human. Wearing clothing over arms and legs will deter ticks as will chemical agents either applied to clothing or directly to the skin. Those who have been outdoors should check themselves in the evening both visually and by sweeping hands over the skin for unfamiliar lumps. Ticks are very small, so diligence is needed. If you find one, DON'T PANIC! It is much more important to remove it effectively than immediately. Ideally you will have tweezers or a card specifically for the purpose, and will deploy these. Using fingernails usually makes the problem worse. Check out gov.uk/government/collections/ticks, which has more information (including how to send your tick in for analysis).

Most large wild animals will retreat from you if given the chance. You will be very lucky to see an adder, and if you do it will probably be speedily hiding itself. The exception is early in the morning, when its cold blood is still sluggish. There are boars in the Forest of Dean. You are most likely to meet a group of females (with extraordinarily cute youngsters) and again, stop, enjoy the moment, and allow them to get away. Don't attempt to feed any animal (wild or domestic) you encounter, including the ponies in the Forest of Dean.

Waymarking

The route is generally signposted from roads by finger-signs. There are also round yellow waymarks along the way. However, these cannot be relied on as the only source of navigational guidance. Maps, GPS and route descriptions will also be necessary to progress.

USING THIS GUIDE

The guide is divided into eight stages, each of about between about 15km and 20km in length. The introduction to each stage includes its distance, elevation gain and loss, and a time estimate based on the formula discussed earlier (4km/hr plus 1min for every 10m of height gain). The introduction also discusses transportation and refreshment options and notes

The banks of the River Severn (Stage 3)

any particular points of interest or issue along the way.

Each stage is divided into four or more smaller sections, which begin and end at access points to the way. Where possible these will be close by amenities or transport links, but this is not always the case, so don't assume that a section end will necessarily be an unplanned termination point for the day. Only the May Hill summit section end is not accessible by car (although there are lanes close by).

Place names in the text that appear on maps are shown in bold. Points of interest along the way are highlighted, and in some cases brief information is given.

It is not expected that the through walker will stick rigidly to the stages for each day's walking. Finding accommodation and individual preference will determine daily progress. This does mean that planning the journey before setting off is likely to be important.

Using this guide is unlikely to be sufficient for navigation. You are advised to complement this with a map (electronic or printed) and, ideally, a compass is recommended. As noted, waymarks along the route are helpful, but are not intended to provide continuous guidance and so cannot be relied on for navigation.

Cicerone app and GPX files

This book is available in the Cicerone app on your phone. View GPS-enabled maps you can download for offline navigation, check route details and local points of interest, and plan your adventure with confidence. GPX files are also available to download. See cicerone.co.uk/1294.

THE GLOUCESTERSHIRE WAY

Huge skies around Condicote (Stage 7)

STAGE 1

Chepstow to Parkend

Start	Old Wye Bridge, Chepstow
Finish	Mary Rose Young Gallery, Parkend
Time	5hr 30min
Distance	19.1km (11.9 miles)
Ascent	430m
Descent	305m
Maps	OL14: Wye Valley & Forest of Dean
Refreshments	None on route. The Rising Sun, Woodcroft; The Rising Sun, Woolaston; The Rising Sun, Bream; Fountain Inn and Woodman Inn, Parkend
Public transport	Buses: between Chepstow and Lydney, and on along the A48. Buses also run from Bream to Lydney. Trains: between Chepstow and Lydney; Dean Forest Railway runs from Lydney to Parkend
Accommodation	Chepstow; St Briavels (4km off route); Parkend

The ancient border town of Chepstow, with its castle and strategic position on the River Wye provides an excellent backdrop for the start of this walk. This section climbs from the tidal reaches of the Wye through gentle farmland and into the Forest of Dean. Some of the smaller coppices and woodlands on the way still feel mysterious and magical, and the homesteads and farms are dispersed and sometimes isolated. But the evidence of human activity and its influence on the landscape is everywhere. As height is gained, there are spectacular views of the Severn from its estuary to the meandering loops higher up in Gloucestershire. Parkend and accommodation is a further 1.5km from the stage end. An alternative is to continue another 5.3km to the Speech House Hotel.

Chepstow (Wye Bridge) to Tidenham Tunnel — 2.4km, 45min

From the old **Wye Bridge**, where the centre panels mark the boundary between Wales and England, walk up Old Hill, directly ahead.

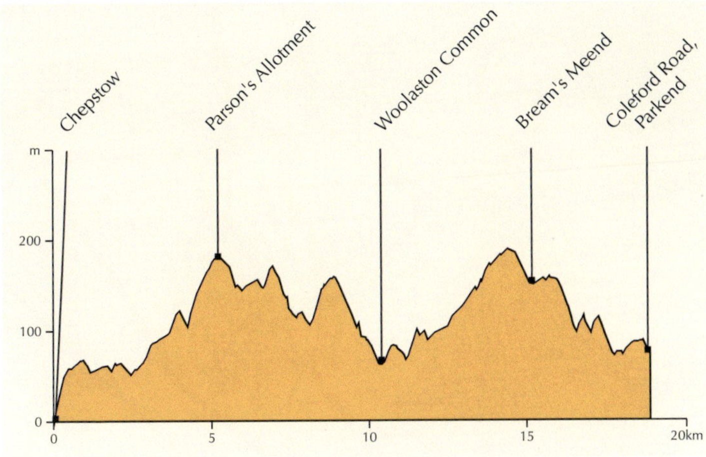

The foundations of Chepstow Castle were laid only a year after the Norman Conquest, being the southernmost stronghold along the Welsh Marches – the wild border with England.

Off and into England!

The old **Wye Bridge** is the lowest point at which the River Wye could be easily bridged, and is where larger seagoing vessels could harbour, to transfer goods to smaller river craft. Bridges have spanned the river here since Roman times; the current iron bridge was designed by John Rennie, who also built London Bridge. This was the only vehicular crossing of the Wye at Chepstow until the Severn Bridge was completed in 1966 and subsequently the A48 bypass in 1988. Several other long-distance paths start here: the Wye Valley Walk, the Wales Coast Path and the Wye Valley Greenway.

Halfway up the hill, **Offa's Dyke Path** joins briefly. Cross a road and continue up Mopla Road (where Offa's Dyke departs) to its junction with the **B4428**, Coleford Road. Continue for 200m and turn right into Elm Road and immediately left onto a footpath between gardens. Cross the old sandstone stile into fields and continue to a cast-iron kissing gate where you turn quarter-right and cross the field. Cross Bishton Lane, taking the right-forking path towards Bishton Farm.

Take the footpath behind the farm and, on meeting a stony track, angle left, uphill. When you reach fields, bear right and follow the field boundary for 250m until you get to a large open gateway, where you turn left to follow the lane for about 230m. To visit the Wye Valley Greenway and Tidenham Tunnel (open April–September) walk on.

Tidenham Tunnel to Ash Grove — 3.2km, 1hr

Just before the old railway, turn left into a field and follow the right boundary, parallel with the Greenway for 450m to reach Netherhope Lane. Cross leftwards to the green lane going uphill. On reaching a field, continue to the kissing gate ahead. Cross the next three fields close by the left-hand boundary until you reach an old orchard and, through this, a track.

Turn right and continue down a lane for 250m into **Boughspring**. After a lane on the right, take the footpath on the left going uphill, emerging after 200m into fields. Look back: the views over Chepstow and the wide Severn are worth a moment.

Jubilee Stone (not much of a view these days!)

Continue in the same direction (north), picking up a hedge on the right. After 250m, pass through a kissing gate next to a field gate, and take the middle of three paths ahead (north). A further 300m and you will reach a crossing track with a stile into woodland, where you fork right. After 210m you will reach a crossing track.

A few metres to the right is **Jubilee Stone**, installed in 1897, the year of Queen Victoria's Diamond Jubilee. The views of Gloucestershire and the River Severn are now occluded by trees.

Over the track, after 170m, take an easily missed right-hand fork, and continue through Parson's Allotment to a road, which you cross to the lane ahead (if it's not straight ahead, turn right to find the junction).

Ash Grove to Woolaston Common

4.1km, 1hr 5min

Walk (north) 600m to the lane end and continue onto an enclosed footpath. Cross the scrubby field close by the right-hand boundary. On meeting a track, err left to re-enter woodland. After 170m, cross a forest road, slightly right, pass a paddock, and at the **Park Hill** road, turn left.

After 140m, take the footpath sharp right into woodland, rounding an old quarry, to a field where you follow the right-hand boundary. In the next field, turn half-right and go downhill to the far corner. Cross over the stile, go down a green lane to a stony farm-track and turn right.

After 110m go through the kissing gate on the left with steps to a holloway descending to the valley bottom. Turn right, and follow the valley for 300m, as it curves leftwards through two fences. With Slade Farm ahead and left, angle left up the slope towards a far kissing gate, which joins the driveway. After 300m, at

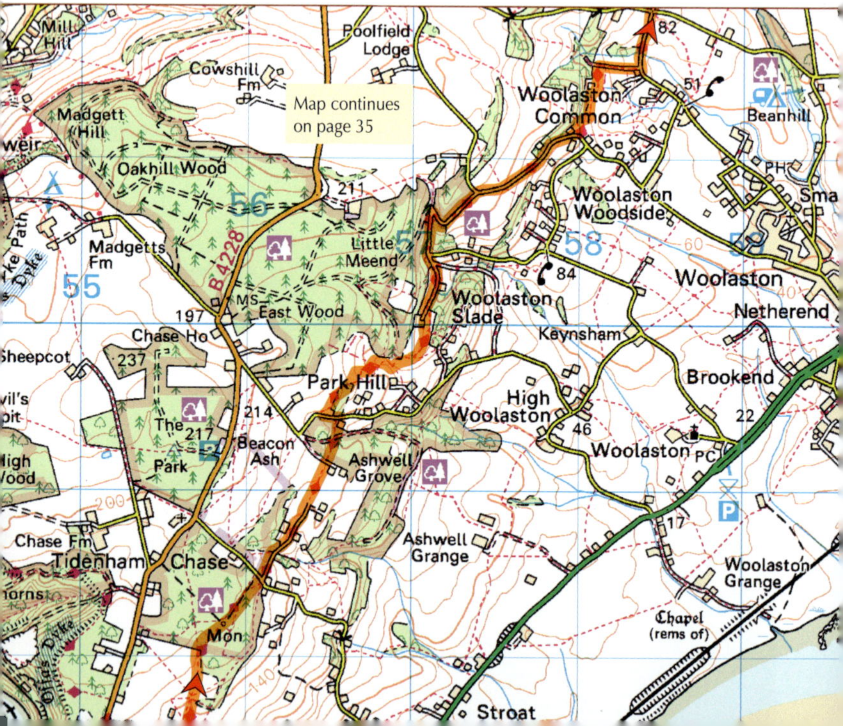

The Old Severn Bridge

a lane, turn left and, shortly, turn left onto a track uphill (north) into woods (avoid the lesser track going south). Continue, passing through a hairpin bend, for 660m.

THE RIVER SEVERN

As height is gained, there are breathtaking views of the Severn and the Cotswolds escarpment. At 354km, the Severn is Britain's longest river, rising in the Cambrian Mountains in Wales, running first northeast, before turning south and passing the three ancient county towns of Shrewsbury, Worcester and Gloucester. In 1826, the Gloucester & Sharpness Canal (26.5km) was constructed to bypass the tortuous stretches and big tides of the River Severn's lower sections. Craft are returned to the river at Gloucester.

On the night of 25 October 1960, two tankers were swept into the Severn Railway Bridge (north of Sharpness). Five crewmen perished and the bridge was severely damaged and subsequently demolished, never to be replaced, sundering the link between east and west Gloucestershire.

From Gloucester, the Severn remains navigable to Stourport. Canals here and at Worcester take traffic into the English Midlands. There is a Severn Way, from source to sea.

The route reaches a lane: turn right and walk 750m. When the lane turns sharp right to **Woolaston Woodside**, turn left into woodland.

Woods near Clanna

Woolaston Woodside to Clanna — 2.2km, 40min

After a short distance fork right, descend for a few metres, then turn to contour the hill northwards. Pass a series of oaks – remnants of an old boundary – with the slope slightly steeper to the left. After 150m, the path turns sharply right downhill, to a stream, where you bear left, uphill again, with a derelict building visible through trees. Find the path beneath this building and cross a paddock to a gap in the hedge ahead. Continue straight (north) until you reach a green lane and turn right. At the metalled lane, turn left, walk 370m to a crossroads and then continue for a further 420m to parking spot on the right, where the Gloucestershire Way enters **Clanna Wood** – a good place for a breather. Note the red-coloured soil, underfoot. The manor house was demolished in the 1950s, and the parkland was purchased by the Forestry Commission.

Pass over two small bridges, and at a crossways, take the uphill path straight ahead (north). On reaching a double-fronted cottage, turn right downhill onto a narrow path. When you emerge into a field, follow the right-hand boundary to **Rodmore Lane**. Turn right, and after 100m take the footpath left into woods. Here is a good place to depart for YHA St Briavels; youth hostel aficionados might stop for a night at this 800-year-old castle.

Clanna to Bream Tufts

3.8km, 1hr 5min

After 40m, fork right, to contour through **Rodmore Grove** for 1.1km (ignoring steep paths leading right, downhill). Here, fork left, maintaining a gentle descent for 230m north to **The Warren**, where you finally meet the stream which you cross several times, before the path diverges right, uphill. Reaching a field, turn left, recross the stream over a bridge and walk left of two ponds, whereafter curve hard right and up the embankment to a stile. Turn right and follow the fence to a track into the yard at **Willsbury Farm**. Immediately, turn left onto a concrete drive.

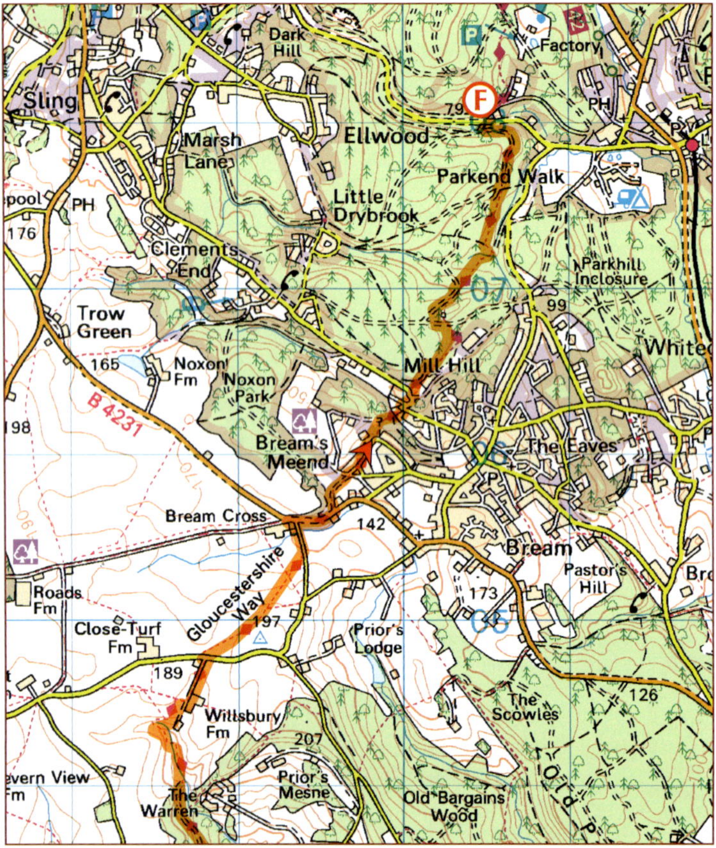

Walk 300m to an old toll house on **Bream Road**, where you turn left and shortly take a footpath on the right into fields.

Turn three-quarters right and cross to a gap in the hedge. Here, angle towards the furthest left-hand corner. Gain this and, in the next large field, with Bream ahead, continue the same line downhill, diagonally crossing towards a hidden gate in the far corner (passing through an intermediate fence near the bottom). At the lane turn left, shortly reaching the **B4231**, where you turn right and, with care and caution, walk 330m to the first house (Bream End) on the right.

Bream Tufts to Mary Rose Young Gallery, Parkend **3.4km, 55min**

Take the track opposite, which shortly curves right over open ground, reaching a sealed road (turn right here for **Bream** pub and shops). Cross over the road to the lane, heading downhill. Where the lane bears right after 250m, a path continues steeply downhill beneath power lines, reaching a driveway and then a lane. Carry on downhill to a turning area, to the right of the lane.

Take the footpath left going uphill. When you meet a wider track, bear right uphill (north-east), soon to level-off. After 400m at a crossing track, turn left, uphill (north-west). After another 90m, you will reach a main crossing track where you turn left (west) and immediately right (north) to crest the hill. At a T-junction, turn right (north-east) downhill along a main vehicular track. After 160m, bear right off the main track onto a smaller path through a firebreak, descending to a cleared strip with electricity lines overhead. Cross over a bridge, turn right (east) and, after 80m, now at the valley bottom, don't cross Oakwood Brook, instead turn sharp left (north-west) into woods.

After 60m, fork right (north) and rise away from the valley. After 400m, you will meet a crossing vehicular track, where you turn right to continue in a northerly direction. Follow this as it curves leftwards (west) and goes downhill. When you meet another track, turn right, and you will soon reach the busy **Parkend to Coleford** road.

Mary Rose Young gallery near Parkend

STAGE 2

Parkend to Boxbush

Start	Mary Rose Young Gallery, Parkend
Finish	Box Bush
Alternative route	To Boxbush via the Wysis Way
Time	5hr 25min; alternative route: 5hr 15min
Distance	18.8km (11.7 miles); alternative route: 18.2km (11.3 miles)
Ascent	420m
Descent	410m
Maps	OL14: Wye Valley & Forest of Dean
Refreshments	The Fountain Inn and The Woodman Inn, Parkend; Beechenhurst Cafe (off route); Forest of Dean Cycle Centre Cafe (off route); Speech House Hotel; Cinderford (off route); Mitcheldean (on Wysis Way alternative); The Yew Tree, Puffely Takeaway and The Forest Bakehouse, Longhope; Farmers Boy Inn, Boxbush
Public transport	Buses: Regular buses (No. 24) from Speech House to Cinderford, Mitcheldean and on to Gloucester. Trains: Dean Forest Railway Parkend
Accommodation	Coleford; Longhope; Mitcheldean; Upper Boxbush

This stage involves idyllic forest walking before visiting more hilly, open country towards the end, when views open up over glorious English countryside. Diversions into Cinderford or Mitcheldean are optional, but otherwise few settlements are visited en route. A glance at the map will show many alternative routes through the forest although on busy days it can be preferable to avoid the cycle paths. The forest cafés noted above are off the route.

Parkend to the Speech House Hotel — 5.6km, 1hr 40min

Proceed up the driveway beyond the **Mary Rose Young Gallery**, crossing the Coleford–Parkend cycleway. Go straight, noting the post made from repurposed railway track; and the colour of stone underfoot: now white limestone. Tungsten steel was first produced in Dark Hill Ironworks, west of here. Goods could be hauled to the Severn by tram and train.

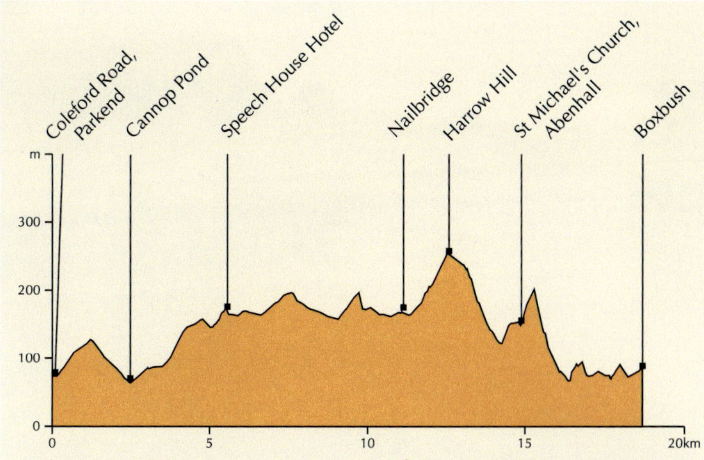

THE FOREST OF DEAN

The Forest of Dean has long been the preserve of monarchs, used for their hunting and for the provision of game. Throughout its history there has been an interplay and tension between conservation and exploitation for industrial and commercial gain. The forest sits above coal-bearing rocks underlain by limestone which outcrop at the rim. The limestone contains iron-ore. There are sandstones in the north. This geology has fostered industries of iron production, coal mining, stone quarrying and glass making. Timber has been used for charcoal and for construction and ship building. Surface coal once supported a cottage industry of extraction, although in the Industrial Revolution this was overtaken by deeper mines.

Efforts to preserve and replant the forest began as long ago as the 1660s, when 'inclosures' were planted and the rights of common usage forfeited. The choice of tree for planting has changed through the years, with conifers predominating during the 19th and 20th centuries, before a practice of balancing conifer and broadleaf plantation was developed in the 1970s. The changing composition of the trees as one passes through the forest is as much a result of centuries of planting decisions as of natural processes. Commercial exploitation of timber continues, although now balanced with environmental preservation.

Cannop Pond

After a short distance, fork left onto the path. Then, 470m further on, take the rightmost of the two paths ahead. After another 600m, cross a wide track and continue due north. This is **Nagshead Plantation** – idyllic woodland walking through mixed broadleaf trees.

After a further 1km, turn right at a forestry road, and continue downhill, crossing a road and passing Forest of Dean Stone Firms Limited towards **Cannop Pond**, formerly a reservoir for the Parkend Ironworks. Bear right over the sluice, and continue until you cross a cycleway, where you take the hand gate ahead up into woodland.

Stone has been quarried in Dean for centuries. The stone used for buildings was mainly Old Red Sandstone and Pennant Sandstone, which can be shaded grey, blue or red. In the 19th century, with the advent of steam power, Parkend became a centre of the stone trade: stone troughs and cider presses were a major product.

In 500m, just after leaving a conifer plantation, turn left (north) at a cross track. Then, 620m further on, take the wide track to the right (east), up the hillside. Continue over the first cross track, and after 630m, at a junction of five tracks, take the second from the left (north). After 400m, fork left onto a lesser (muddier) track.

Continue for another 500m before crossing over a ditch and dyke boundary. Follow the path towards a hardstand for parking and the **B4226**, but just before take the path on the right, which filters through trees and scrub, parallel to the B4226, to reach the **Speech House Hotel**. Built in 1670 as a keeper's lodge, Speech House was leased from the Crown as an inn in 1841. It still hosts meetings of Forest Verderers and Free Miners.

Speech House Hotel to Nailbridge (A4151) — 5.6km, 1hr 30min

Standing in front of Speech House cross the B4226, walk directly into the woodland for 40m and turn right onto a track. Walk 600m past picnic areas and

Map continues on page 43

Forest of Dean Sculpture Trail

car parks on the right, and a modern sculpture on the left. The Forest of Dean Sculpture Trust has installed 18 sculptures along an 8km trail; the GW passes two of them.

Beyond the car park, take the track bearing left (north-east) and, after 450m you will pass a pond on the right. In a further 450m, go through a wooden gate and carry straight on (north-east). After 300m, take the left fork, converging with the fence around a conifer plantation. Go through the gate at the crossing fence, and continue downhill (north) passing over a muddy crossing track to reach a dry forestry road. Turn right and shortly left, passing Drybrook Road Station after 150m. Drybrook Road Station (1875–1944), on the Severn and Wye Railway line, used to be the stop for Cinderford, until closer stations were opened.

Walk 20m further north, where two parallel paths go right (east): the first is better – on the raised old tramway. At a fork after 500m bear left. (Straight on for Cinderford.) Shortly after, take a path left (north), uphill into woodland. Crest the hill after 580m and, 180m further on, you will meet a forestry road.

The route is straight on through a clump of trees, but it can be easier to walk round this. Find the forest track northwards and, after 100m, opposite a derelict brickworks, turn right through a wooden gate into Hawkes Well Plantation. The path meanders close to the right boundary until after 700m, at a crossing track, you turn left and, 400m further on, you reach the A4151 at **Nailbridge**.

Nailbridge (A4151) to Longhope — 5.3km, 1hr 35min

Cross the **A4151** slightly left, to round the corner of a house and go over scrub and ahead up a driveway to a metal gate. Take the stile to its left. Follow garden boundaries, then cross a garden, angling right through the old railway embankment. Pass into woodland and continue north-west until you reach the wall around a large lawn; keep left (east) and reach its top corner, where you cross a small track and then bear left (north) through woods to the busy **A4136** Gloucester–Monmouthshire road.

Turn right, walk 100m and cross the road to a path. Head directly uphill, north-east, through Harryhill Plantation, cresting the hill after 500m. The track bears down, slightly right, continuing for another 500m east-north-east, to a road. An alternative route from here to Boxbush via Mitcheldean is described at the end of this stage.

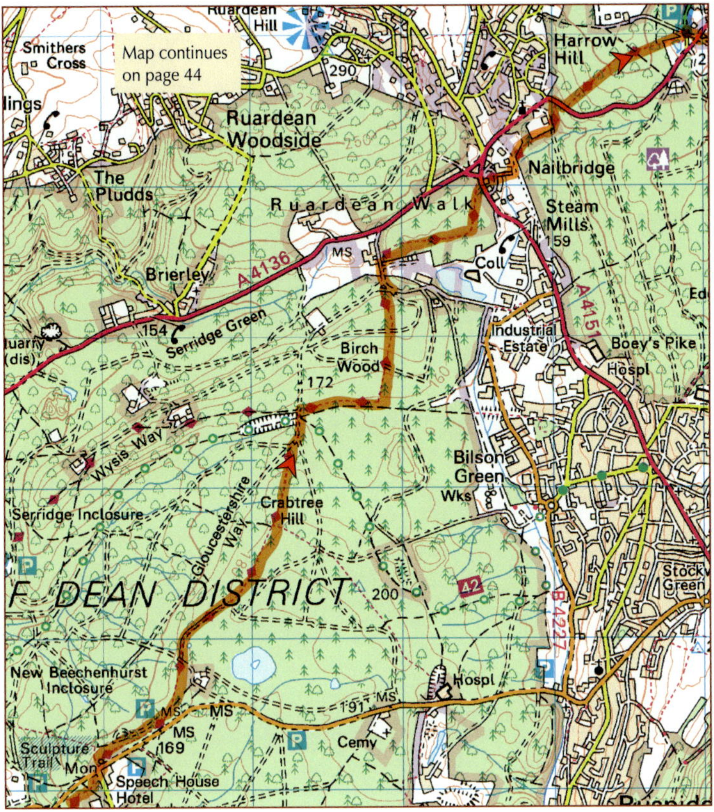

Alternative route map continues on page 47
Lea
Knightshill
High Hope
dismtd rly
Lea Line
Yartleton Fm
May Hill
296
May Hill Ho
The Rock
Dursley Cross
The Rudge
East Dean
Boxbush
PH
F
Lyndors Fm
Bradley Court
Wysis Way
Bilbut Fm
B4224
Court Fm
Hobbs
Wigpool Common
Chessgrove
Business Village
Breakheart Hill
219
Longhope
Mitcheldean
Craft Centre
Water Wks
A 4136
Brimps Hill
Folly Fm
Sch
Gloucestershire Way
Pool Hill
The Wilderness
Hope Wood
Drybrook
Plump Hill
Abenhall
Harrow Hill
Hazel Hill
Blaisdon Hall
Gaulet
Flaxley Woods
The Rookery
Shapridge
Nailbridge
Furnace (rems of)
Steam Mills
Welshbury Wood
Green Bottom
Flaxley Abbey
Edge Hills
Industrial
A 4151
Grove Fm

St Michael's Church, Abenhall

Continue ahead and cross the A4136 rightwards, to the small lane marked 'The Rocks and Hazel Hill', taking the left fork almost immediately. After 300m, at a junction of roads, continue downhill on the road ahead. Presently, fork right, but immediately take the footpath left going downhill by a stream, emerging after 400m onto a lane. Turn left, walk 50m past Green Farm and turn right into a restricted byway which crosses the valley, bearing left to a road. Take care! The sight lines here are poor. Turn left and, after 150m, right into Church Lane. Abenhall church celebrates the work and industry of the Forest of Dean.

Pass St Michael's Church, **Abenhall**, stay on the lane where it turns right and, after 50m, take the footpath up steps. Cross the first field keeping by the right hedge. In the next field, angle left and find the pond on the hill crest – a good place to pause and view. The industrial complex on the edge of Mitcheldean was the European production site for Xerox machines from 1960 to 2002.

Go downhill keeping the left boundary close by, maintaining this line through and out of a strip of woodland. Just before Whitmore Farm, take the stile on the left to the farmyard, where you turn left. Just past buildings take the footpath right through brush. In the field, go downhill through the gate ahead, then orientate towards the left of the trees on May Hill (Stage 3), soon to pick out the stile in the hedge. Here turn slightly right to the track that leads to Marshes Farm and exit onto a lay-by on the A4136. For Longhope pub and shops, turn right, and then left into the village. After 2km rejoin the route.

Longhope, where ploughed fields can be bright red.

Longhope to Boxbush **2.3km, 40min**

Cross, to the footpath opposite, and go steeply uphill to a stile, where you bear right. At the top boundary cross into an enclosed track around the hillside which bears right and descends to a meeting of tracks. Turn left and follow the driveway until it turns into a property, where you bear right onto a footpath. Cross two fields keeping to the left-hand field boundary. Pass over the lane and cross a larger field, maintaining the same line.

Exit onto a lane, turn right and, 50m after a tight bend, take the path on the left over a stone footbridge. Cross the next field to a lane, where you turn left and walk 100m to steps up the bank on the right. Cross the field downhill diagonally, passing an oak, to its far corner where there is a hidden exit. Those who diverted through Longhope village, rejoin here.

Turn left and walk along Church Road to its junction with the **A40**. (The Farmers Boy Inn is about 580m further along the A40.)

Alternative route to Boxbush (A40) along the Wysis Way **5.4km, 1hr 30min**

This alternative route from Harryhill Plantation is 600m shorter and 10 minutes quicker. Having emerged from Harryhill Plantation turn left along the minor road.

Bear right with the road, ignoring the first left footpath, for 250m and take the path left. After 570m, as the path descends, go right to a gate in the boundary. Cross the field towards the summit of May Hill (Stage 3). Go over a stile and follow a boundary wall to a second stile, where the path curves left alongside a hedgerow. Now follow this line downhill to **Mitcheldean**, with its conspicuous church spire. Pass into the churchyard and then out onto the High Street, **B4224**, and turn left.

Walk 600m to a junction by the business park where you fork right onto the minor road – this road is busy; care and caution needed. Walk 500m, passing one footpath, to a second path on the right by a house. Walk up 240m to a cross hedge, enter the field on the left and ascend diagonally to a track. Go uphill, passing to the left of **Bilbut Farm** to crest the ridge. Descend directly ahead into the valley, aiming for the single remaining gatepost in the porous hedge. Beyond, make for the stile directly ahead, by a kink in the boundary. Go through the stile, keep on the same line uphill, with a hedge on your left. Presently this is crossed, but continue uphill, hedge on the right, to the crest.

Continue to follow the boundary, which bears slightly left, downhill, passing close to three oak trees to a stile under ash trees. Aim to the left of a white cottage and emerge onto the A40 at **Boxbush**. To reach the end of Stage 2, turn right and walk about 375m to the junction with Church Road. To continue to May Hill (Stage 3), turn right, and then take the first road left. To reach the Farmers Boy Inn, turn left.

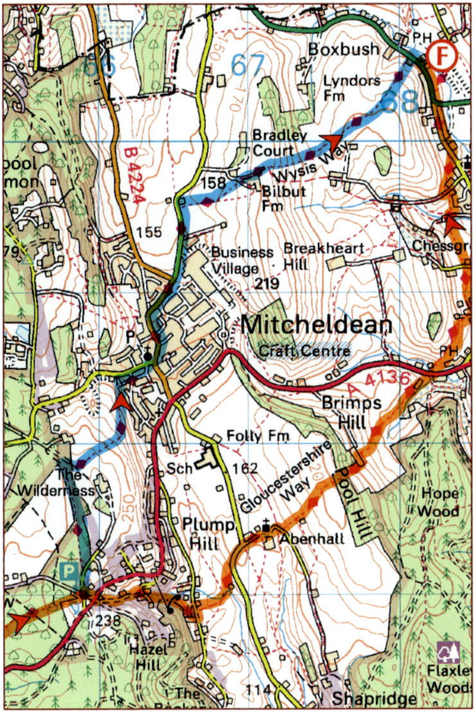

STAGE 3

Boxbush to Gloucester

Start	Boxbush
Finish	Gloucester (Severn pedestrian bridge)
Alternative route	Along the River Severn (Severn Way/Geopark Way)
Time	5hr 35min; alternative route: 6hr 30min
Distance	20.5km (12.7 miles); alternative route: 24.2km (15 miles)
Ascent	250m
Descent	325m
Maps	OL14: Wye Valley & Forest of Dean, Explorer 179: Gloucester, Cheltenham & Stroud
Refreshments	Glass House Inn, Glasshouse (off route); Leaf Creative garden centre and The Red Lion Inn, Huntley; The Fairview Gardener (tearoom) and Kings Head pub, Birdwood; Over: Over Farm, Toby Carvery and The Lock Keepers; Gloucester
Public transport	Buses run along the A40 from Huntley and along the A48. Onward transport at Gloucester
Accommodation	May Hill; Huntley; Minsterworth; Over; Gloucester

This stage starts with the short, steep ascent of May Hill, revealing its spectacular panorama. The walk passes through the last fragments of the Forest of Dean and then over attractive farmland before reaching the River Severn, which is followed to Gloucester.

Boxbush to May Hill summit — 2km, 50min

(Those setting out from the Farmers Boy Inn should walk south for 150m and take Barrel Lane on the left, which shortly rejoins the main route.)

Starting from the junction of Church Road and the **A40**, walk 150m (north) to stand in front of the Nags Head Inn (now closed). Cross to the old pub car park and take the kissing gate (directly opposite the entrance) into a field where you angle left to a footbridge. Cross the old railway embankment and, shortly after, turn right at Barrel Lane.

View from May Hill – Sugar Loaf

Map continues on page 50

Take the first right up a metalled bridleway past houses. Watch for the footpath on the right, up steps and into a holloway. On reaching large ash trees, turn half-right and diagonally cross to a handrail and steps. Cross the next field uphill to a clump of trees, and filter through, slightly right, to another stile. Follow the fence uphill to May Hill Farm, where you continue on the footpath up to a lane. Turn left and after a few steps turn right continuing the ascent of **May Hill**, straight up to the tree-covered summit.

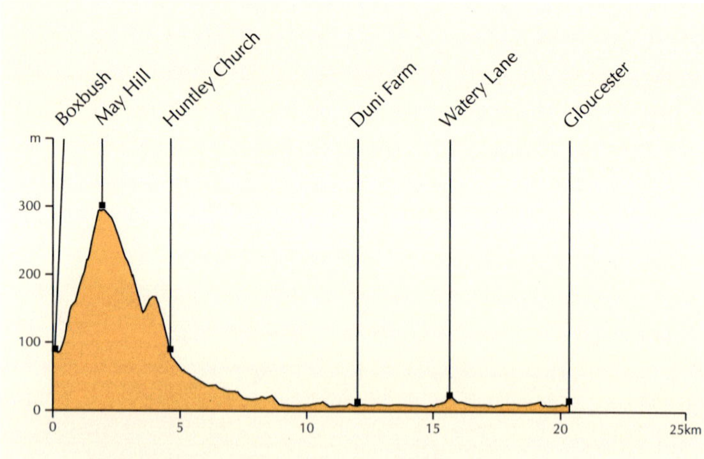

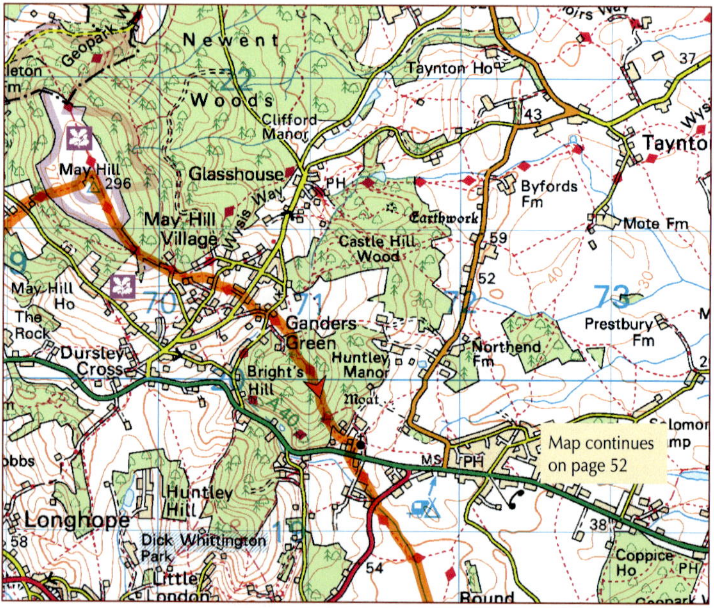

Map continues on page 52

May Hill to Longhope Road (A40) **2.8km, 45min**

At the trig point, with the summit plantation behind, the track descends southeastwards towards the distant Severn, picking up mixed woodland on the left. Apart from a short section round Bright's Hill, the Gloucestershire Way is now coincident with the Geopark Way to the Severn.

May Hill at 294m is the highest point in Gloucestershire, west of the River Severn (and the high point of the Gloucestershire Way). Looking east it's usually possible to discern the communication masts atop Cleeve Hill, which stands at 330m. To the west is the distinctive cone of Sugar Loaf, near Abergavenny. And to the south is the Severn estuary. The summit plantation contributes to May Hill's distinctive profile.

Old sawmill chimney – coming down May Hill

At a crossing of paths in front of a house, carry straight on and, 80m further, continue straight downhill (the Wysis Way, forks left towards the Glasshouse Inn 1.2km). Sixteenth-century Flemish artisans, fleeing religious persecution, settled here, finding the raw materials they needed (sand for glass, timber for fuel).

After 120m, fork left and, 170m later, turn right at a lane and immediately left on a path downhill. Cross the next lane right to a stile. Cross two fields, in the second angling to a gateway right of the red stone house, where you bear left to the lane at **Ganders Green**. The red-brick chimney in the right of the field is what remains of a steam-powered sawmill.

Cross to the enclosed pathway, going uphill to a field. Continue just left of a clump of trees towards the woods ahead. Enter the woods at the gateway and continue 870m over **Bright's Hill** and then down to reach steps by **Huntley** school and church. St John the Baptist Church hosts a 1500-year-old yew tree, split near the ground. Turn right here (or left through the churchyard to visit the ancient yew and garden centre café) down the short driveway to reach the busy **A40** Gloucester–Ross-on-Wye road.

The Huntley yew

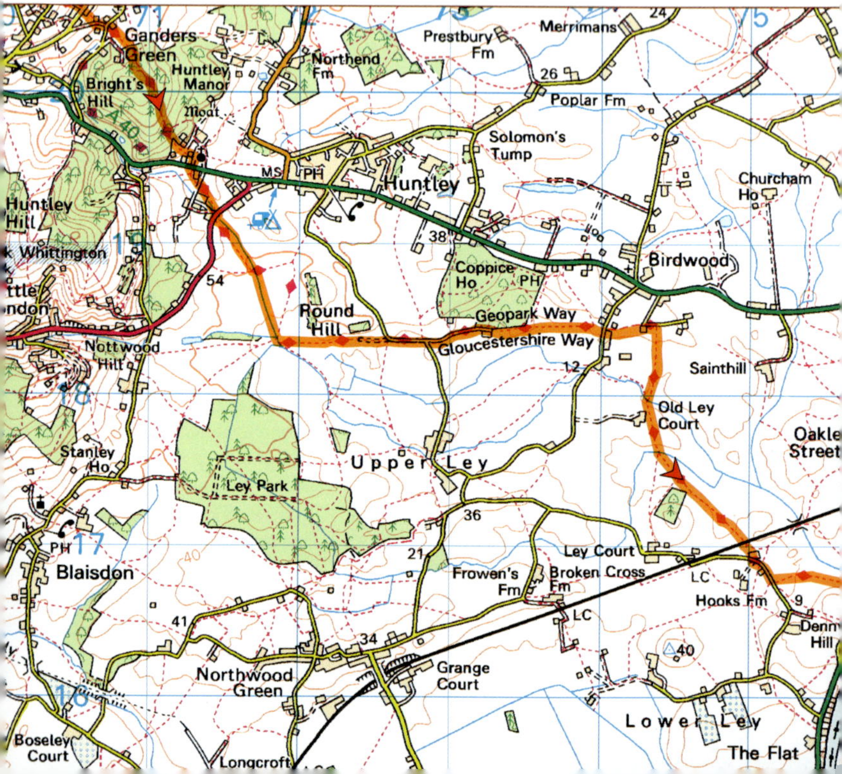

Longhope Road (A40) to Birdwood **3.5km, 55min**

Cross the A40 to a stile and go through the field along the left boundary to a driveway. Cross the driveway, turn half-right and walk low over the shoulder of the hill to a gateway onto the **A4136** Gloucester to Monmouth road.

Cross to the right, and keep ahead, following a stream on the left for 470m, to a footbridge, which you cross. If possible, follow the right-hand boundary by the stream. However, the official right of way goes straight ahead to the far boundary, turns right for 100m, then turns half-right to recross the field diagonally to the stream in the far-right corner. Exit the field and turn left. (The GW now proceeds due east for 2.6km.)

Walk 800m over three large fields along the left-hand boundary to a lane. Continue for 250m, to a driveway, straight on, into Whitlow Farm. After 320m, just before the farm, take the stile on the left into a paddock. Bear right and walk through a series of paddocks, with woods on your left. When the woods end (unless diverting north to the King's Head pub) cross the large field by the right-hand boundary to reach **Birdwood** (The Fairview Gardener tearoom is to the north).

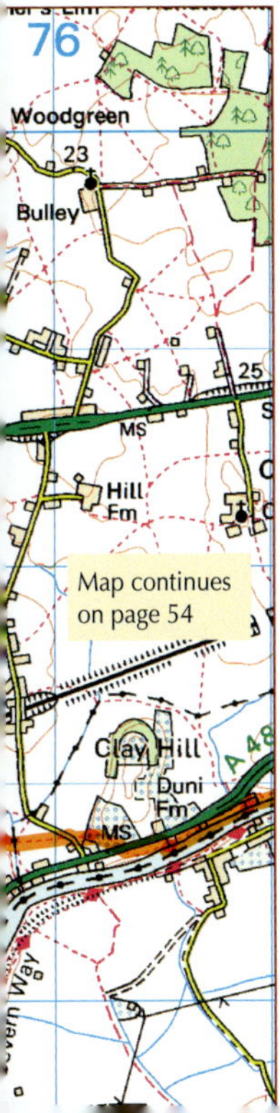

Map continues on page 54

Birdwood to Duni Farm (A48) **3.6km 55min**

Cross the lane to a bridleway and then onto a lane, where shortly you will turn right into fields. Follow the left side of the hedge running away ahead. In the next field head towards the brick buildings of **Old Ley Court** and cross Ley Brook. Cross the next field diagonally left, orientating towards the high point of Ley Court Wood, ahead. Take the right of two field gates and, having crossed a stream via a concrete bridge, immediately turn left into the next field through a hand gate. Follow the right-hand field boundary for 200m. This time, ignore the field gate and find the stile a few metres further on. Cross diagonally left to the far-side boundary which you follow through a crossing boundary. Maintain this line, cutting across the right corner of scrubby field to the far corner stile. Here bear right to reach the railway line.

Cross with caution. Turn immediately left, cross a stile and turn right into Green Farm, passing between buildings to a lane. Turn left and, ignoring the first footpath, after 200m turn left into fields. If the path has been ploughed in, orientate left of Denny Hill ahead. Cross a ditch via a bridge and continue, with **Denny Hill** kept well to the right. Over the shoulder, look leftwards for the substantial footbridge in the far boundary. Here, go ahead towards the telegraph pole in the furthest corner. On

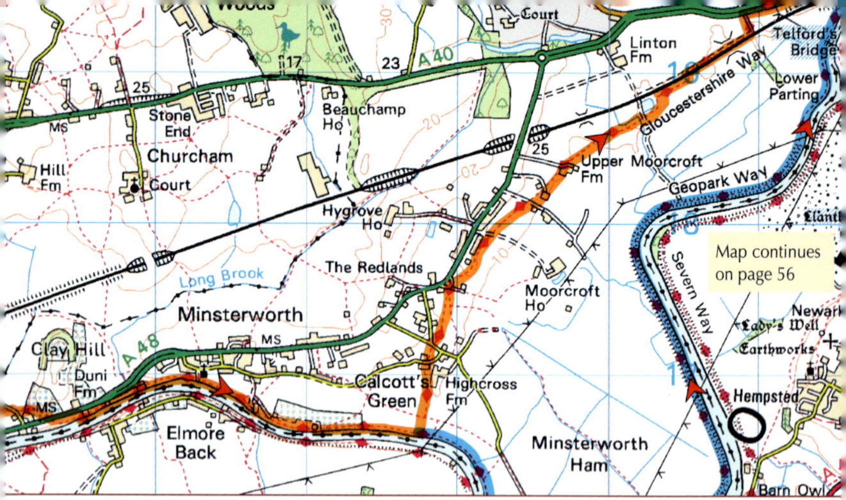

its left a stile gives onto a lane. Turn right and shortly left into a driveway, "Cherry Orchard", and take the footpath right of the gates. Exiting into an orchard, bear right round a right angle of garden boundaries and proceed to the gate onto the **A48** Gloucester to Chepstow road, west of **Duni Farm**.

The Gloucestershire Way passes **ancient apple and pear orchards**, some sadly neglected. Old varieties had wonderful names: Skyrmes Kernel, Dymock Red, Forest Styre, Black Foxwhelps and Redstreak.

Duni Farm (A48) to Watery Lane (A48) — 3.7km, 55min

Cross the A48 and turn left, following the pavement for 230m, until a path leads up to the Severn riverside. Pass behind Severnside Cottage, descend to a lay-by, and walk on to a fork where you will soon regain the riverbank. After 400m pass **Minsterworth Church**, then continue for 1.55km to a field with power lines ahead. Local poet, FW Harvey, is buried in Minsterworth. "Forest and vale and high blue hill" is a line from his poem, 'A Song of Gloucestershire'.

The **Severn Bore** is the racing wave that moves up the river as the rising tide is funnelled by the Bristol Channel into the narrowing river. The highest bores, which can be surfed upstream for many kilometres, occur at the spring tides around the equinoxes, but lesser examples occur throughout the year. The banks here are an excellent viewing point.

Crossing into the field with power lines ahead, turn left directly away from the river, to a stile (the right of way is actually along a sluice at the far side of the field, but this short-cut is well established). The Severn riverside (Geopark Way/ Severn Way) can be followed all the way to Over (Telford's Bridge). This will add 3.7km/55min to the route. Continue along this line, over a dyke, a footbridge, a field and left of a garage to a lane. Cross the stile opposite to a field, then follow the left boundary to another lane. Take the footpath opposite, pass through two small fields and then a third larger one, and aim for a protruding hedge corner and the exit onto the A48 at The Redlands.

Watery Lane (A48) to Telford's Bridge — 3.7km, 55min

Immediately turn right and climb over a stile into a well-maintained garden, which you cross left of a pond to a kissing gate. Spot Gloucester Cathedral, almost directly ahead.

Turn half-left, cross the paddock to a stile, and turn left to pass through a narrow field. In the wide field beyond, turn half-right, pass close to a mature oak and go over the metalled track to a stile in the boundary. Now aim for the furthest telegraph pole, sighting a hand gate as it is neared. Pass through the gate and maintain this line through a scrubby field to a bridge over a stream by another telegraph pole.

Walk directly ahead, passing a farmhouse to a gate and, in the field beyond, aim towards a gate on the left of **Upper Moorcroft Farm** buildings. Walk over a metalled lane and cross the following field by the right-hand boundary to a bridge.

Oak in field after Watery Lane

Keeping the same line, cross the next large field towards a protruding right-angle in the far boundary, 320m away. Pass the woods on your left and then a bund which you follow round left to the railway embankment. Turn right and follow the railway to a stile on the left. (Underpasses shown on the OS map are not accessible.) Cross the railway with caution. Turn right, walk 500m and turn left to the **A40** Gloucester to Ross-on-Wye road. Cross the road to get to Over Farm, Toby Carvery and The Lock Keepers. Turn right, walk 950m and cross Over "Telford's" Bridge.

Designed by Thomas Telford, copied from a bridge over the Seine, **Over Bridge** was opened in 1831. The arch sank ten inches due to subsidence when the scaffolding was first removed. Telford was apparently confident the bridge was safe, and he was right: the bridge was only retired from traffic use in 1974.

Gloucester Cathedral

Telford's Bridge to Gloucester (Severn Pedestrian Bridge) **1.2km, 20min**

Having crossed the west branch of the Severn onto **Alney Island**, turn right and, after 20m, the Gloucestershire Way is signposted left, soon picking up the railway line. After 250m pass under the **A417** and then into fields. After another 200m, turn right under red-brick arches carrying the railway and go through the ornamented kissing gate celebrating the Millennium and Gloucestershire Way! Take the track ahead through trees and exit onto the A417, which you follow until a footpath forks off to the left. Take the minor road ahead, staying parallel to the A417, and walk to a path which goes under the main road and then cross over Westgate pedestrian bridge, leaving Alney Island. For the city and cathedral, turn right, pass under the road and turn left up to the pavement. Follow for 450m to a pedestrian crossing.

GLOUCESTER

Gloucester was developed by the Romans (as Glevum) and has been an important city ever since. Its situation on the major navigable river of western England is akin to that of London in the east. In 1089 William the Conqueror held court here, giving instructions for the creation of his Doomsday Book. The centre of the city has a number of attractive medieval buildings, but the crowning glory is the cathedral, which is one of England's finest. Within is the tomb of King Edward II who was murdered in nearby Berkeley Castle.

STAGE 4

Gloucester to Shurdington

Start	Gloucester (by Severn pedestrian bridge)
Finish	Shurdington (A46)
Time	4hr 20min
Distance	16.5km (10.3 miles)
Ascent	90m
Descent	8m
Maps	Explorer 179: Gloucester, Cheltenham & Stroud
Refreshments	Gloucester; The Queens Head, Longford; Brickhampton Golf Club (check first) and Hare and Hounds (1km off route), B4063; The Old Elm Inn (1.6km off route), Churchdown; The Dawn Nurseries, The Greenway Hotel & Spa and The Cheese Rollers, A46
Public transport	Buses run from Gloucester along the A38, through Longford; also along the B4063 through Brickhampton and on to Cheltenham. Buses also run along the A46, passing Shurdington and on to Cheltenham
Accommodation	Twigworth; Down Hatherley; Churchdown (off route); Shurdington (off route); Cheltenham (off route)

This stage crosses the Severn Vale from Gloucester to the bottom of the Cotswold escarpment. The Gloucestershire Way, as routed, only bypasses the City of Gloucester, but most walkers undertaking the whole way are likely to delay here, to visit the cathedral and other city delights.

The route starts by following the navigable River Severn for several kilometres out of the city and then finds quiet paths to cross the flatlands through farms and rural hamlets. This stage has little in the way of ascent, and is shorter in distance than other stages, which allows time for dawdling, visiting Gloucester or Cheltenham, or progressing into the Cotwolds.

Junction of Base Lane and Sandhurst Lane

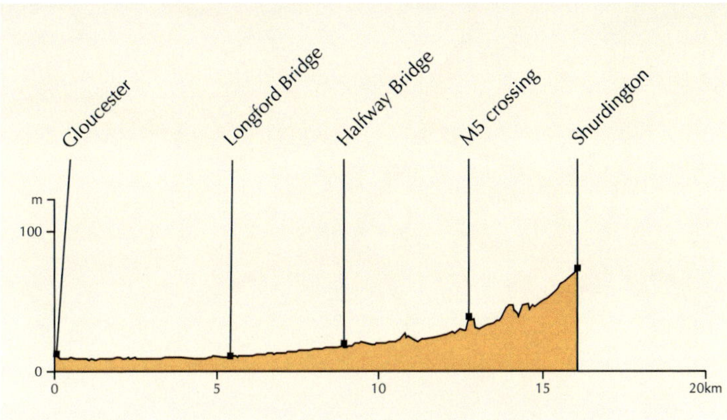

Gloucester to Longford Bridge (A38)

5.3km, 1hr 20min

> After many years without maintenance, in 2025 **the path along the east side of the Severn** was cleared and is once again passable. Check the Cicerone website to ensure this remains the case. This is the most pleasant of the many routes out of Gloucester – it's a quiet walk along the riverbank.

From the east side of the Westgate pedestrian bridge (SO 82469 19034), facing Gloucester city, turn left (north) and follow the river upstream for 2.5km to the sturdy flow gates at **Horsbere Brook**, where the path is directed onto Sandhurst Lane (SO 82866 20875), where you turn left.

In the case of the riverside route not being available (which includes time of flood and high spring tides), the most direct alternative is to walk along the A417,

Map continues on page 63

Gurney Window in Gloucester Cathedral (credit Gloucester Cathedral)

St Oswald's Road, to its junction with Sandhurst Lane (SO 83447 19741) and then proceed left along the lane for 1.3km to reach Horsbere Brook.

From Horsebere Brook, walk 670m along Sandhurst Lane, where you fork right. After a further 330m, turn right onto a footpath between oak trees. Cross the field by the left-hand boundary to a gate in the far fence, and then maintain the same line over the next field, to the right of a lone willow. Ascend the rise ahead, keeping a nearby pylon well to the left (orientating towards another pylon in the middle distance). Soon you will spot the bridge over Broadboard Brook. Carry straight on towards the pylon on the far side of the field and exit onto the A38 at **Longford Bridge**. Churchdown Hill is visible in the middle distance with the Cotswold escarpment beyond.

IVOR GURNEY

Ivor Gurney (1890-1937), poet and composer, was born in Gloucester and is buried in St Matthew's Church, Twigworth (525m north of Longford Bridge), where there is a small memorial. There is a stained-glass window to his memory in Gloucester Cathedral. His poetry and songs celebrated nature and the county from which he came. Sadly, emotional fragility was compounded by his experiences in World War I: initially his output continued, but lessened as ill health overwhelmed him.

East Wind

Cool air moves there up on Cotswold edge,
By Crickley's bastion or the Shurdington wedge,
Grey grass rustles, the harebells dance and the East
Wind has no good influences on the cattle at feast.

Naked land-slides show, away downhill mist-shades cover
The land where South-West once moved high like a lover,
With colour and boy's glory and breath of renewal:
That also, that valley, for this dry air is a fuel.

But the great steeps keep one in right hoping still,
Mighty the upstanding curving of the golden-crowned hill
Crickley, where scabious and serious thistle nods,
And there is good hiding place for the old gods.

Ivor Gurney

Longford Bridge (A38) to Halfway Bridge (B4063) — 4.5km, 1hr 10min

Cross the busy **A38** directly to the footpath and then cross the field diagonally, to reach **Hatherley Brook** (to be followed for 3.5km) at the far left-hand corner. Cross a large and then narrow field by the brook. Exiting the second field, turn hard left and cross a concrete bridge over a ditch. Follow the path next to the brook for 1.8km, exiting onto Frog Furlong Lane.

Cross left to the wooded footpath into the **Brickhampton Court Golf Course** and follow Hatherley Brook on the left. Don't take any of the left turns crossing the brook until, 1.75km from the golf course entrance, you reach a small wooden footbridge next to an old brick culvert. Cross the brook and continue walking another 400m, with what is now Norman's Brook on your right, until you reach the **B4063** Gloucester to Cheltenham road at Halfway Bridge.

Halfway Bridge (B4063) to Churchdown (M5 crossing) — 3.4km, 55min

Turn right along the B4063, walk 100m and cross to the footpath which follows the airport perimeter fence for 1.5km, to eventually run parallel with the busy **A40**. Gloucestershire Airport is a busy General Aviation airfield. Take the underpass, which bears right to fields, then take the left gate into the field, and follow the boundary (and A40) westwards, back to Norman's Brook, where you turn left, through fields, with the brook on your right.

Cross Hatherley Brook in Brickhampton Court Golf Course

From the left turn, continue for 700m, pass over a concrete farm track (or turn right here if going to Churchdown) and continue towards the right of Home Farm ahead. Pass through two kissing gates and cross a field diagonally right to a **railway underpass**. Go under the railway line and cross the next fields, initially converging with the **M5**, then diverging to a concrete farm bridge and up a small hill to Brookfield Road.

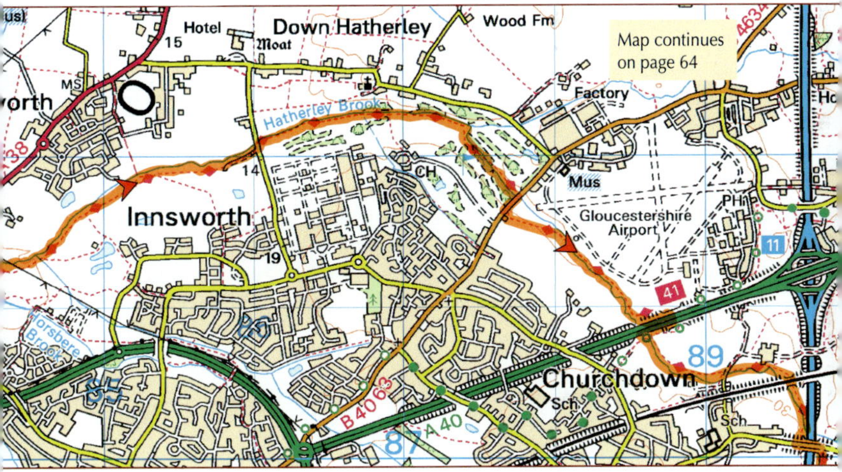

Map continues on page 64

Churchdown (M5 crossing) to Shurdington (A46)

3.3km, 55min

Turn left, cross the bridge over the M5, to a footpath on the right. Walk parallel to the M5 for 120m along a green lane, then turn left through a kissing gate and cross the field diagonally right (walk round the boundary if cropped) to a kink in the boundary. Turn left and follow the path by Norman's Brook through fields and paddocks to a footbridge, where you climb a field to a lane. Step five paces right to the enclosed path into **Badgeworth** churchyard where you turn left to the lychgate.

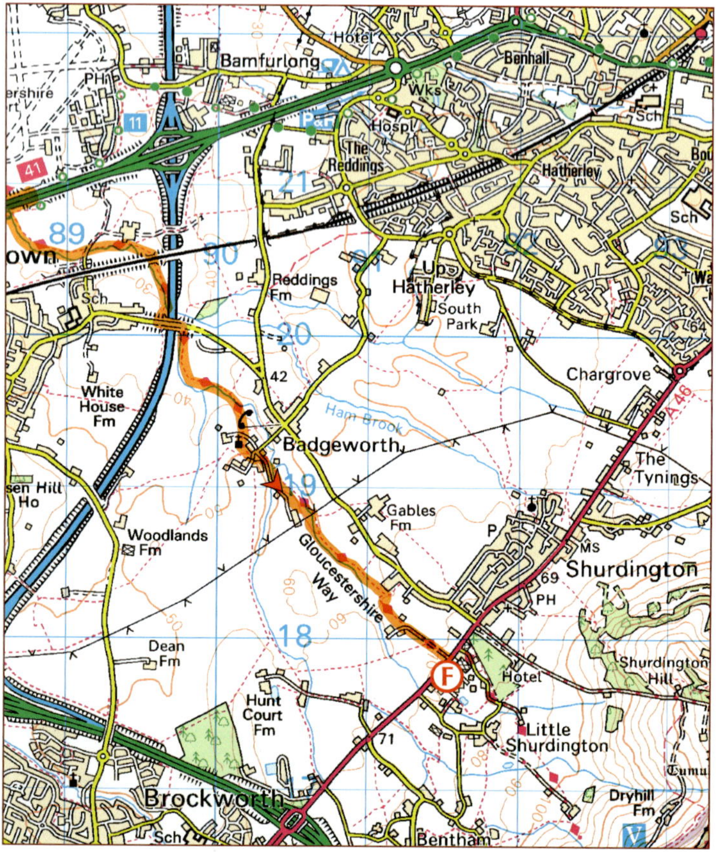

Churchdown Hill

Out of the churchyard, turn left downhill past the green and then turn right onto a driveway. Where this bears right, continue into the field ahead by wooden garages. Rise slightly and continue with brooks on both right and left. From the field entrance, continue for 320m and, with a gate ahead, drop down left to the brook, cross a footbridge and emerge into a field where you turn right. Walk for 700m by the brook towards red-brick houses. Pass into an enclosed track by a garden fence and, after 80m, recross the brook via a bridge. Continue for about 50m away from the stream, before turning left to a green lane by a hedge. The Cotswold escarpment looms ahead. Continue along a track until you reach the **A46** Cheltenham to Stroud road.

STAGE 5

Shurdington to Shipton Oliffe

Start	Shurdington (A46)
Finish	The Frogmill, Shipton Oliffe (A40)
Time	4hr 40min
Distance	15.6km (9.7 miles)
Ascent	440m
Descent	330m
Maps	Explorer 179: Gloucester, Cheltenham & Stroud; OL45: The Cotswolds
Refreshments	Crickley Hill café; National Star College, Ullenwood (2km off route); The Royal George Hotel, Birdlip (2.5km along Cotswold Way); Cowley Manor, Cowley (1.5km off route); The Green Dragon Inn, Cockleford (2.4km off route); The Frogmill, Shipton Oliffe
Public transport	Regular bus services along the A46 from Shurdington to Cheltenham and Gloucester. Less frequent services from Coberley (A435) and Shipton (A436) to Cheltenham
Accommodation	Ullenwood/Crickley Hill; Birdlip; Cowley; Cockleford (all off route); The Frogmill/Shipton Oliffe

The climb up Crickley Hill is in every sense breathtaking. There's no shame in pausing to look behind for the views as they open up over the wide Severn Vale. A short detour will earn a coffee stop at the very top. Then you enter the rolling hills of the Cotswolds, traversing a series of ridges and passing through a succession of quiet villages and hamlets, built from the iconic and much-prized Oolite Limestone. This is a landscape of meadows, peace, quiet and long views. There are no shops en route, and a single public house, The Frogmill, just before the A40 crossing.

The A417 at the start of the route is subject to a major Highway's Agency project which will result in two pedestrian bridges being installed, one of which will be planted with hedges to encourage its use by wildlife. On completion (hopefully in 2027) the line of the Gloucestershire Way will actually be little changed, but in the meantime be ready for some minor diversions.

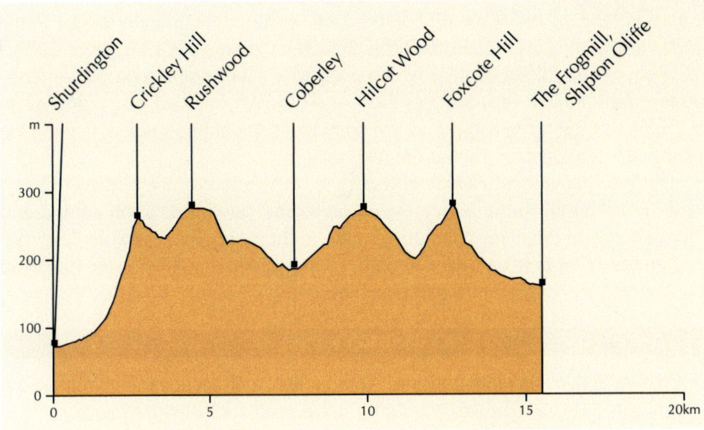

Shurdington (A46) to Crickley Hill **3.7km, 214m ascent, 1hr 15min**

Turn left and then first right by Dawn Nurseries on Whitelands Lane. Follow this for 500m, to the second right-hand bend where you continue into a driveway. Before the cottage, turn right onto a footpath that runs by the garden fence. Reach a field, which you cross diagonally left, and then either cross, or walk around, a couple of paddocks to a stile. Walk up the hill towards a gap in the field boundary, then continue towards Greenfield Farm. The path exits onto a lane in front of the house, where you turn left and pass through the farmyard, going uphill past the last building.

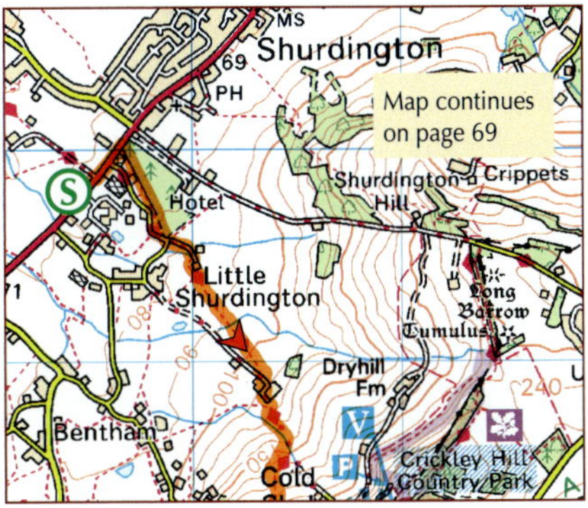

Turn right on a track, through a boundary, then left uphill on a ridge in a narrow field with streams either side. The path is on the left-hand side, going uphill to a boundary, marked only by ash trees, where you cross over to a stile. Cross the next field at a softer angle to an old stone stile. Turn half-left, cross the field diagonally and go through porous hedges with a new stone house above left. Continue to a metal barn and take the old stone stile onto a lane. Keep turning around to take in the wide view of the Severn Vale. Spot the 'Doughnut', home of GCHQ since 2004.

Turn left to a flight of steps which leads to a minor ridge, soon with a fence on the right. Follow this, to meet the Cotswold Way, marked by a signpost (at SO 92541 16096). The two routes run coincident downhill, loosely following the right-hand boundary for 1km to the **A417**.

An alternative on **Crickley Hill** park is to turn left on the Cotswold Way, walk 600m uphill to the high viewing point and café/information centre, and then find one of the many alternative routes to the A417. The Cotswold Way runs 165km from Chipping Campden to Bath. For the most part following the Cotswold Escarpment, it is met again at Winchcombe.

CRICKLEY HILL

Crickley Hill has a violent history, with evidence of occupation going back as far as 3700BCE. The first Neolithic settlement, a causewayed enclosure, occupied about 4 acres of high ground, surrounded by a double ring of banks and ditches. There is evidence of a second Neolithic settlement and a battle around 3550BCE as well as a cairn, mound and sacred circle dating from 2000BCE. The Neolithic structures were abandoned until the construction of an Iron Age hill fort around 700BCE. Further Iron Age and Roman settlements were constructed until the settlement was once again abandoned following a battle in the sixth century BCE.

Meeting the Cotswold Way on Crickley Hill

Crickley Hill to Coberley

3.7km, 1hr

The Air Balloon pub pulled its last pint on New Year's Eve 2022 and was demolished the following year, as part of the A417 development. A pub stood here for centuries, gaining its name in 1802 after the pioneering balloon flights that took place off the escarpment.

Old route

Having reached the junction of roads, you will need to contrive, with care, to reach the east side of the A417 as it rises up the hill towards Cirencester, possibly crossing directly to the path into Emma's Grove, 150m from the roundabouts. Curve right and up through the wood and exit where walkers are marshalled by fences up the hill, through boundaries, to a metalled road heading south-east towards buildings (expect diversions).

New route

On completion of the A417 project, take the pedestrian bridge over the A417. Walk 150m north (coincident with the Cotswold Way), uphill, along the line of the old road, now a cycle and equestrian way. Continue 150m up the hill and take the footpath left into woodland, Emma's Grove. Curve right and up through the wood, then exit to a path which you will follow uphill.

Continue up the hill until you reach the 'environmental' bridge over the A417. Cross over and turn right, walking parallel with the road. At a junction, turn right, bringing you close by the A417 for a short distance to a metalled lane, where you turn left towards buildings.

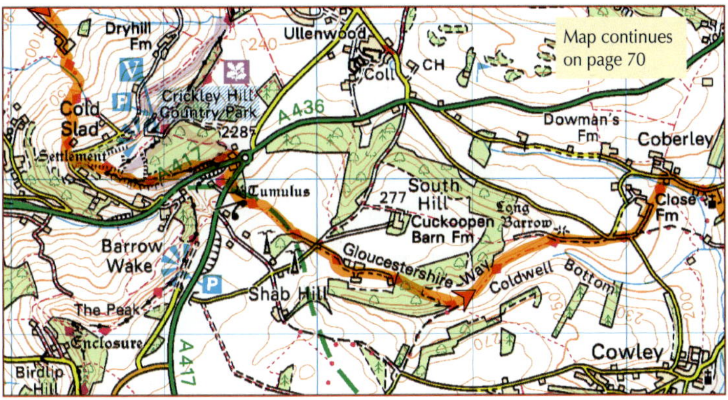

Coldwell Bottom

Main route

With the environmental bridge (or its construction site) behind you, pass Rushwood Kennels (due for demolition) on the left and follow the track east-south-east into an enclosed footpath. As you descend, the view opens. With the valley bottom below, ahead, just before a gate turn left onto a green lane, which contours around Coldwell Bottom for 1.1km. When you reach a lane, turn right.

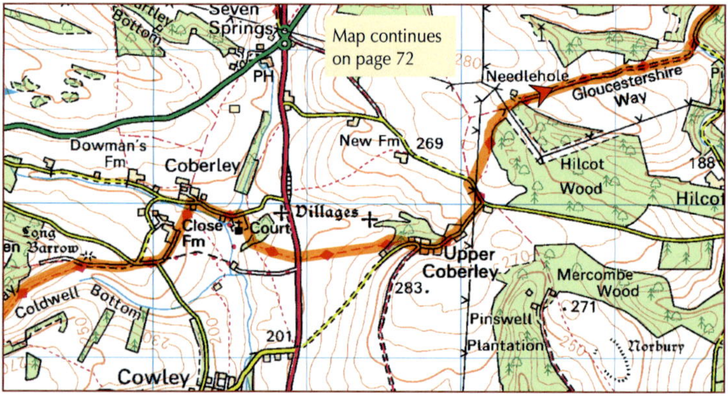

Map continues on page 72

Walk for 150m to where the road bends right and bear off left onto a track then immediately fork left to follow the path to **Coberley**, where you turn right.

Coberley to Foxcote

6.6km, 2hr

Walk 350m, crossing the infant River Churn, past **Coberley Court** and the entrance to the church, and take the path right alongside buildings. Continue past ponds to a gate. Go through the gate, turn half-left and orientate towards the high point in the hills ahead, crossing the field to a hidden gap onto the **A435**. Cross with care and follow the bridleway 500m over the field to woods. Enter the woods and head up to a lane at **Upper Coberley**, where you turn left. *Downhill to London. The high Cotswold escarpment is a watershed between the Severn and the Thames. The Churn, Coln, Windrush, Eye and Dikler are all tributaries of the Thames.*

Walk 750m through this pretty hamlet, turning left at a T-junction, until you find the path at a knuckle in the road, on the right near power lines. Walk to the left foot of the pylon then towards the leftmost corner of woods ahead, going through the crossing boundary hard by the woods. Turn left and follow the woodland boundary to the driveway by **Needlehole Cottage**.

Follow the driveway for 1.2km to a lane, where you turn left and walk 1.1km to crest a hill. Take the footpath right, initially with a fence on the right, but shortly pass through this, and continue with it on the left. Descend towards an electrical pole and, soon after, head for a track and gateway.

Upper Coberley

THE COTSWOLDS NATIONAL LANDSCAPE

The Cotswolds was designated an Area of Outstanding Natural Beauty in 1966. This is still its legal designation, but the term 'National Landscape' was adopted in 2023 to reflect the importance of such areas and stress their national value. It was also considered useful to develop commonalities of branding and management. There are 46 such areas in the country. The CNL is the largest, at 2046 km², extending from Bath in the south to Chipping Campden in the north.

Turn left along the track and, after 200m, take the path half-right, which angles diagonally across fields, around a paddock and towards woodland. Pass through the wood and walk through an equestrian establishment to the road at **Foxcote**.

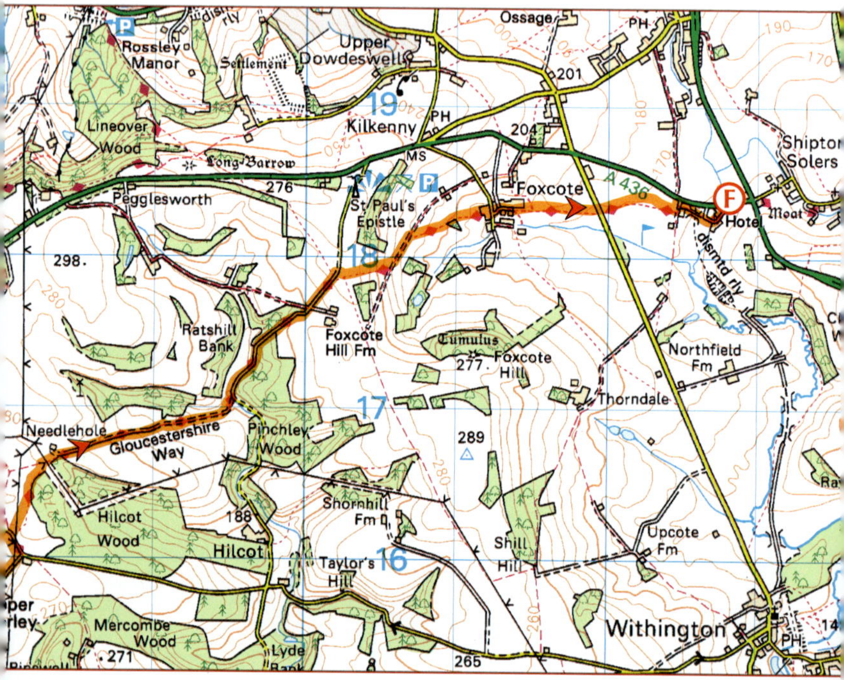

The stream at Shipton feeds the Coln, which in turn feeds the Thames

Foxcote to The Frogmill

1.6km, 25min

Turn right and immediately left, into a cul-de-sac that reaches a field gate. Pass 550m through three fields, staying close to the left boundary, until you reach a road. Cross to the field opposite next to the right boundary by **Shipton Golf Course** and emerge onto a driveway. Turn left and, just before the main road, turn right onto a bridleway, which crosses first the former Cheltenham to Cirencester railway line. Then cross the infant River Coln before reaching **The Frogmill**.

Once a mill, and mentioned in the Doomsday Book, in the 1600s **Frogmill** became a coaching inn. It was the first staging post of the 'Gloucester Flying Machine', a mail coach that could complete the 105-mile journey to London in two days – the express service of the day.

STAGE 6

Shipton Oliffe to Stow-on-the-Wold

Start	The Frogmill, Shipton Oliffe (A40)
Finish	Stow-on-the-Wold
Alternative route	Visiting Bourton-on-the-Water
Time	6hr 10min; alternative route: 6hr 50min
Distance	21.9km (13.6 miles); alternative route: 24.3km (15.1 miles)
Ascent	340m
Descent	280m
Maps	OL45: The Cotswolds
Refreshments	Notgrove Hub, Notgrove; The Plough Inn, Cold Aston; The Slaughters Country Inn and The Slaughters Manor House, Lower Slaughter; Bourton-on-the-Water (2km off route); Stow-on-the-Wold
Public transport	Buses: along the A436/A429 and at Bourton-on-the-Water and Stow-on-the-Wold. Trains: at Moreton-in-Marsh
Accommodation	Cold Aston; Lower Slaughter; Bourton-on-the-Water; Stow-on-the-Wold

This is a wonderful Cotswold section, with grand airy vistas, a series of picturesque villages and magical enclosed footpaths. Most of the way is easily navigated. There are regular opportunities for refreshment and the option to divert to the honeypot that is Bourton-on-the-Water. This is a stage to savour and take time over.

The Frogmill to Salperton War Memorial — 5.8km, 1hr 40min

From the inn, continue to the **A40**. Cross with care and continue towards **Shipton Solers**, but shortly take the footpath to the right. If visiting St Mary's Church, stay on the lane. Pass through paddocks, leaving the last through a hand gate, and here turn left towards a rivulet of the Coln. Turn right and walk over a small bridge, then cross a driveway to a footpath. At the village street, turn right.

SHIPTON

There are two Shiptons: Shipton Solers and Shipton Oliffe, which in medieval times were separate manors. Each has its ancient church, dating from at least the 13th century. In 1666, Joseph Walker, already rector at Shipton Solers, took on that role at Shipton Oliffe, and the thoroughly modern practice of alternating services between the churches commenced. In 1776 the benefices were united and St Mary's in Shipton Solers was designated the 'mother church'. However, St Oswald's in Shipton Oliffe, possibly by virtue of its more central position, appears always to have been preferred, and St Mary's is recorded as having been abandoned a number of times over the centuries. In 1883, Charles Pugh, on becoming rector, found St Mary's in use as a cowshed, with the windows blocked and trees growing through the roof. He restored it, and services recommenced, but it was not long before the church again fell into disrepair. It remained in this state until 1930, when it was restored yet again, this time with the addition of the stained-glass windows. Both little churches are worth a visit.

Walk through this pretty village. After about 630m, at a house called The Lilacs fork left uphill and go straight on at the crossroads, past the Reading Room. The road bears left, uphill, and presently you turn right into North Farm. Follow the track for 1.1km, passing Tottmoor House, and fork left onto a track by an electricity pole. After 500m you will reach a road at Hampen (the farm sometimes

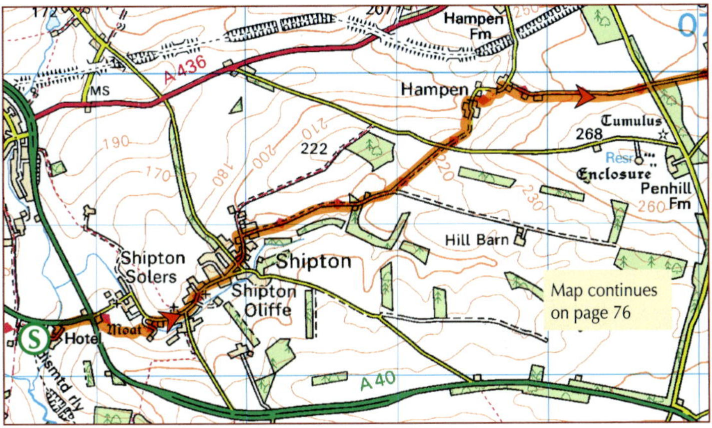

Map continues on page 76

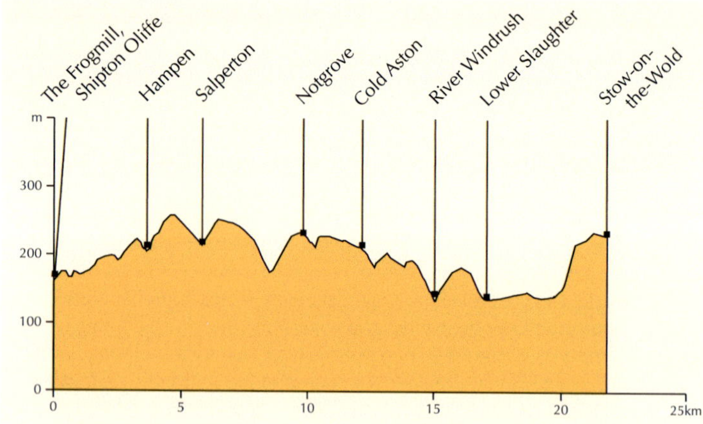

has refreshments). Cross the lane slightly right and walk down an avenue into the secluded hamlet of **Hampen**. Ahead spot the line of Cheltenham to Kingham railway, closed in 1962. The route crosses the line just before Lower Slaughter. Sadly, it has not been repurposed for leisure use.

Fork right into the village, walking between houses. After the last barn, turn right into a field, and err gently left, to cross the path of a stream (usually dry) after 150m and then walk directly uphill to rejoin the lane. Turn right and shortly left round the corner and then take the tree-lined driveway to the right; after the houses it becomes a dirt track. Follow this for about 1km to a junction with a small road. Cross this and follow the road ahead down into **Salperton**. After 900m turn right (south) at the war memorial.

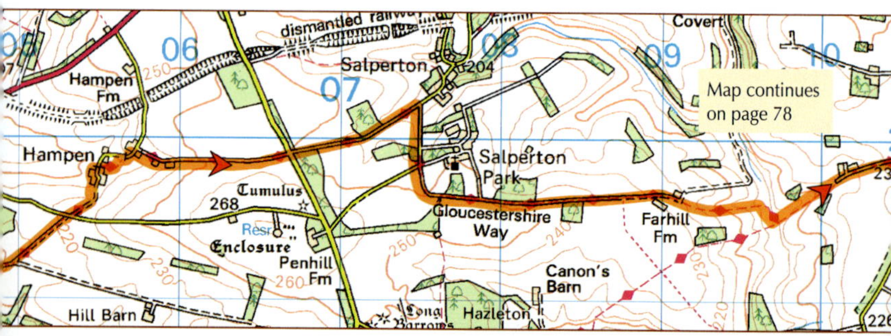

Map continues on page 78

Note the lowered walls, topped with wooden beams, that allow the hunt to pass. Also note the iconography of the **war memorial**, which was erected in 1919 by the Roman Catholic Harter family, then owners of Salperton Manor.

Salperton to Notgrove

4.2km, 1hr 15min

Go up the hill, passing entrances to **Salperton Park** and its neighbouring church.

Salperton – village on the saltway – is mentioned in the Domesday Book; ownership passed from the Saxon Wulfward to the Norman Hugh L'Asne after the 1066 conquest.

The road curves round to the left, and the views open up ahead and to the right. After 2km you will pass **Farhill Farm** and, as the track turns into the farmyard, continue straight on, passing through two fields until you reach the valley bottom. Dry valleys are characteristic of the Cotswolds. Porous limestone rock means water often flows underground and valleys are only wet in winter.

Pass through a gate, turn right along the valley and, soon after, bear slightly left towards an ancient hollow ash. Go through the gate beyond, turn left and follow the field boundary on the left up the hill. Go up through two fields with gates,

Gnarled and hollow ash tree

Cottages in Little Aston

and pass Kitehill Barn, now on a metalled track. When you reach a lane, turn left and after 150m turn right to walk through **Notgrove** village (to visit Notgrove Hub take the first lane on the left). A charming Cotswold village with lovely old houses; the Notgrove Hub serves food and drink.

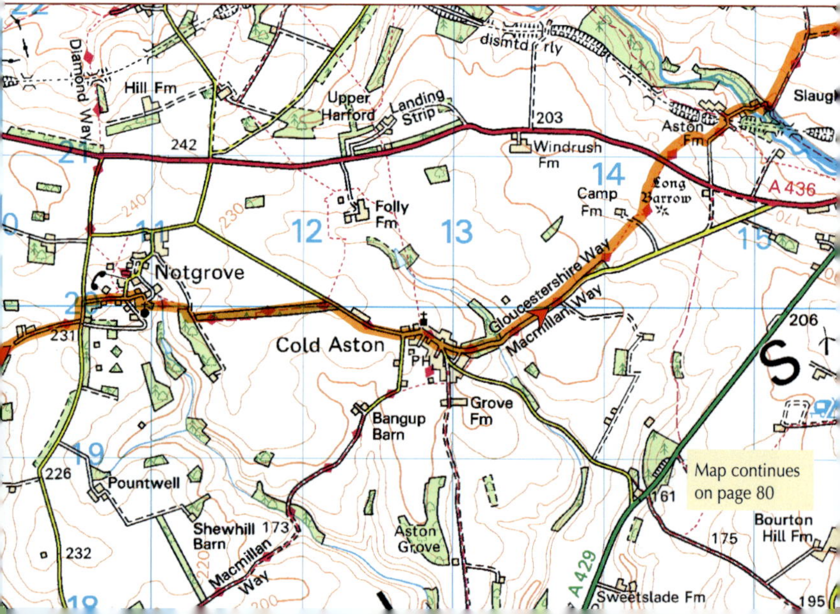

Map continues on page 80

Notgrove to Cold Aston

2.3km, 35min

From the turning to the Notgrove Hub, continue between stone pillars signed 'Manor Farm, Glebe Farm, The Church'. Curve right, past a barn into a small farmyard. (An option is to visit the church, ahead.) Turn left through a field gate. Cross the field, descending into the valley and then ascending the opposite slope to its top right-hand corner. Exit onto a track, turn right, and after about 50m turn left into a magnificent avenue of beech. After 900m exit onto a road and turn right towards **Cold Aston**. In 800m you will reach The Plough Inn.

THE WOOL TRADE

Cold Aston is so-called because of its exposed aspect high on the Cotswold Hills. The name 'Cotswold' derives from *cot* – meaning enclosure or pen – and *wold* – meaning rounded hill. In medieval times the wool trade was a source of wealth both locally and nationally and 'sheep pens on the hillside' reflects the economic activity that sustained this area. The 'Cotswold Lion', a distinctive breed of sheep suitable for these lands, has become the emblem of the area and used as a logo for the Cotswold National Landscape. The fine churches in the local towns are testament to the riches the wool trade generated.

Cold Aston to Lower Slaughter

5km, 1hr 20min

Set off along the road to the left of the huge sycamore tree. After 1.1km you will reach Claylodge Coppice, where the way forks left into a field, but continues in the same direction, with the field boundary on the right. Cross two fields to a track at the valley bottom. Cross the track slightly left to the path going up the hill that again follows the right-hand field edge.

The **drystone walls** here date from the 18th and 19th centuries when land was enclosed for livestock. (The earliest local examples of the iconic walls are at Belas Knapp, a long barrow near Winchcombe, that dates from around 2000BCE.)

Cross straight over the **A436** and follow the right-hand field boundary that, after 260m, curves right and exits onto a lane. Turn left, downhill, go across the line of the old railway and, at an apparent fork with **Aston Farm** to the left, turn right downhill and cross the **River Windrush**. Ascend the hill passing Little Aston Mill and pretty houses. At a fork in the path, turn left to continue up the hillside, with paddocks on your left.

Footpath above Lower Slaughter

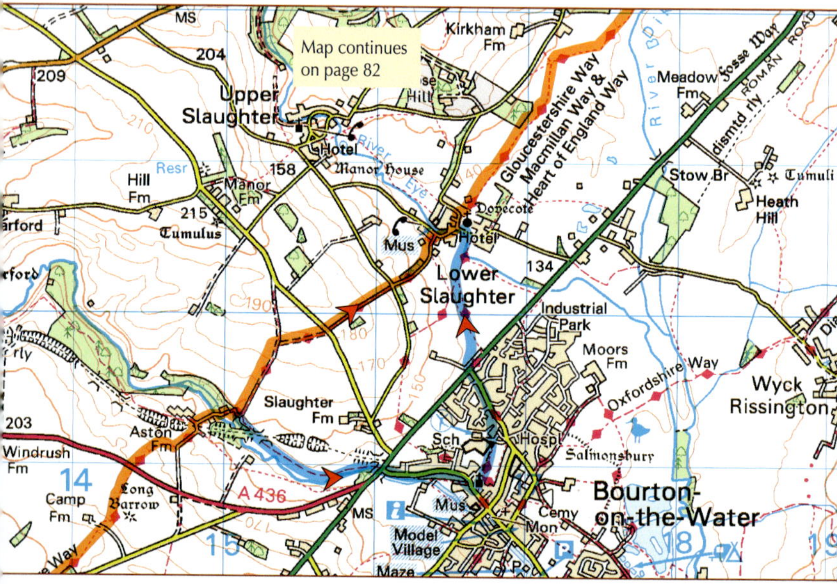

Map continues
on page 82

An alternative here is to take the right fork and follow the Windrush Way into Bourton-on-the-Water (all amenities and lots of tourists!). This will add 2.4km or 40min to the journey.

Some 500m from the fork, pass through a second boundary fence and, 60m further, look for a gateway into a field on the right which you cross diagonally to a minor road.

This is the Roman **Ryknild Street** (known by the Saxons as Buckle Street), which ran from the Fosseway at Bourton-on-the-Water all the way to York. It will be crossed again at Condicote (Stage 7).

Cross the road to a bridleway, shortly cresting the ridge and proceeding downhill. Cross the next small road to the lane ahead down into **Lower Slaughter**. Slaughter, from the Old English meaning 'wet place', suggests a muddy river crossing. Now, with the River Eye tamed and channelled, it's as picturesque a village as one could wish. Turn right in the village to follow the **River Eye** downstream. Note the Old Mill to your left.

Lower Slaughter to Stow-on-the-Wold

4.6km, 1hr 20min

When you reach a road junction, fork left, passing the church on your right. After the churchyard, turn right into a close and shortly turn left to a footpath, passing

The Old Mill, Lower Slaughter

an orchard and cricket pitch. Follow this line for 730m, switching to have the boundary on the left.

With a cross boundary ahead, look for the gap and footbridge about 20m right of the corner (temporary fences or crops sometimes affect the line here). Walk 100m straight ahead to the next boundary, cutting the left field corner. Aim ahead for the steel gate, 250m away, between two old oaks.

Turn half-right, cross a track and walk parallel with the right boundary fence, but err left towards a gap in the hedge ahead. Turn left here and cross another boundary, but then turn half-right and cross the next field diagonally. Three-quarters across, there is an overgrown ditch and bridge, which you cross, keeping the same line until you reach a gap in the hedge. Pass through this and stay on the same line to a gap in the corner of the next field, which is hard by the River Dikler. These fields are a 'Coronation Meadow' – a restoration of flower-rich grasslands. Look out for returning plant life, including several species of orchid. The river meanders away to the right, but the path keeps on straight to a small stone bridge crossing a stream. Cross over the bridge and bear slightly right towards **Hyde Mill**. Walkers wanting to by-pass Stow can take the Heart of England Way north to Lower Swell and on to Upper Swell, where the Gloucestershire Way is rejoined.

Pass by the homestead and buildings, cross a bridge over the millpond and immediately bear left through two hand gates. Cross the field diagonally and climb steps onto a dyke. Turn left, passing a stable and exercise yard, and go through **Nether Swell Farm**, and walk up through fields and a number of gates to a copse. Entering the copse, bear right and exit onto a path that develops into a hard track where continue to the **A429 Fosseway**.

Yews outside St Edward's Church, Stow)

Turn left and shortly cross the road via an island refuge. Walk past the cemetery and turn right into Back Walls. Walk 200m, passing a small Methodist church and graveyard and, just beyond, take the enclosed footpath left. Walk to Sheep Street, cross this to another small alley (Talbot Ture) and continue to the town square.

STOW-ON-THE-WOLD

At 244m, Stow-on-the-Wold is the highest town in the Cotswolds. Its heyday was at the height of the medieval wool trade when it was a busy sheep exchange. Its location was no doubt chosen for its defensible hilltop position, at the crossroads of many existing routes. Walkers will have noticed that several modern routes converge here (Gloucestershire Way, Monarch's Way, Heart of England Way, Macmillan Way). Stow has historically been a market town, gaining charters for both a weekly market and twice-yearly fairs. The latter continue in spring and autumn as the Stow Horse Fairs, although now moved to fields outside the town. Most walkers will stop here, and Stow repays exploration. Don't miss the yew sentinels at St Edward's Church or the small passageways – *tures* – possibly once used to corral and count sheep at market.

STAGE 7

Stow-on-the-Wold to Winchcombe

Start	Stow-on-the-Wold
Finish	Winchcombe
Alternative route	Via Hayles Fruit Farm and the Cotswold Way
Time	6hr; alternative route: 6hr 25min
Distance	21.7km (13.5 miles); alternative route: 23.2km (14.4 miles)
Ascent	300m
Descent	445m
Maps	OL45: The Cotswolds
Refreshments	The Plough Inn, Ford
Public transport	There is no public transport until Winchcombe. Trains: Gloucestershire Warwickshire Steam Railway (GWSR) runs from Winchcombe (see Stage 8 for details)
Accommodation	Upper Swell; Winchcombe

This stage joins the picturesque towns of Stow-on-the-Wold and Winchcombe, crossing splendid upland country. Early sections involve road walking, but on quiet lanes. This is a stage of big Cotswold skies which give way to bucolic scenery descending into Winchcombe. Walkers will experience an ancient landscape, evident in place names, structures and paths dating from from prehistoric, Roman and medieval times.

Stow-on-the-Wold to Upper Swell — 2km, 30min

Leave Stow Market Square, passing the old stocks, by the High Street, returning to the **A429 Fosseway** which you cross via the nearby pelican crossing. Bear left down the **A424** and immediately left onto the **B4077** Tewkesbury Road, which you follow downhill on its left verge for 1.1km. After the entrance to **Abbotswood House**, turn left into a field and follow the left-hand fence down to a stone bridge over the **River Dikler**. Walk up the enclosed field-edge path beyond and turn right into the field at the kissing gate. Loop across the field, initially walking diagonally towards the river, and exit to the road. Turn left up the hill through the hamlet of **Upper Swell**, remaining cautious of traffic.

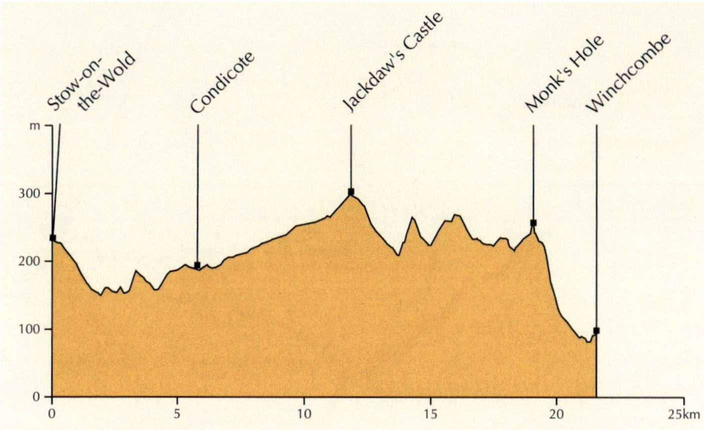

Upper Swell to Condicote

3.9km, 1hr 5min

This is a section of road walking: although the lanes are quiet, remain vigilant. Having turned a sharp corner in the village, 250m later, fork right signposted to **Donnington Brewery**, which you will reach after 800m.

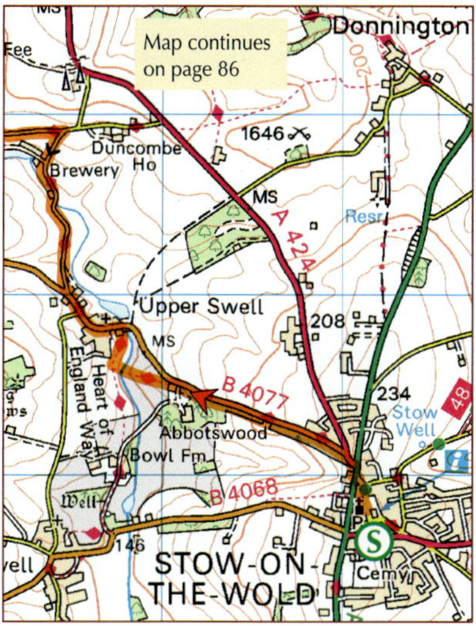

A mill stood here in medieval times. However, in 1827 the freehold and buildings were purchased by Thomas Arkell, and his descendent, Richard Arkell, started brewing beer in 1865. This continues still, using water drawn from a nearby spring, hops from Worcestershire and barley from Norfolk. The **Donnington Brewery** owns a small number of local inns, including The Plough, at Ford, which is on the Gloucestershire Way. Tours of the brewery can be arranged, see donnington-brewery.com

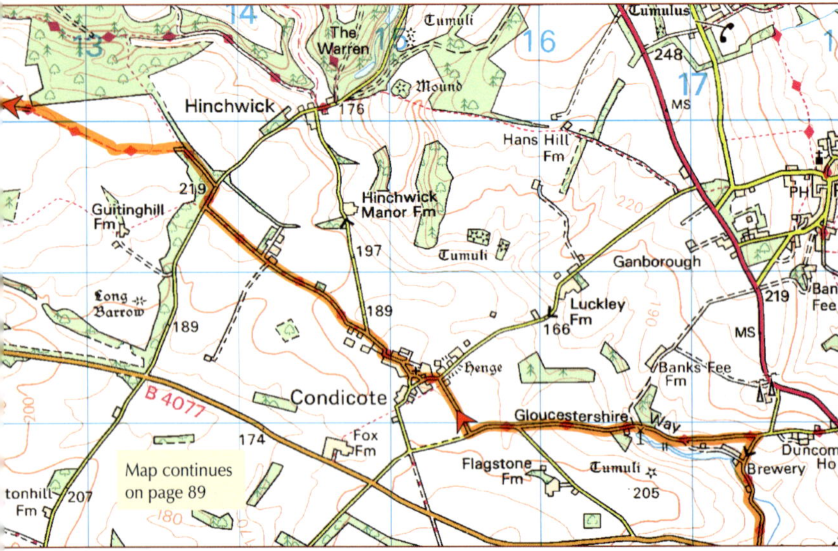

Map continues on page 89

On the lane between Donnington and Condicote

St Nicholas Church, Condicote

Continue 200m to a T-junction and turn left towards Condicote, now walking parallel to the River Dikler. After 2km, take the right turn signposted to **Condicote** and walk 400m where you turn left into the village.

St Nicholas Church, **Condicote**, is believed to date from the 11th century. On the village green is a wayside cross, set beside a spring, which no doubt has sustained both inhabitants and travellers through the ages. This is an ancient landscape, which has been rich in finds from Neolithic and Bronze Age times. Ryknild Street (see also Stage 6) runs through the village, but it is certain the Romans were utilizing a route established in prehistory.

Condicote to Ford

7.6km, 2hrs 5min

Take the right fork in front of the village green, pass the church of St Nicholas on the right and then turn sharp right. Walk through the village for about 500m to where the road turns right (along the line of Ryknild Street) and here bear off left along a metalled track. Follow this for 1.4km, passing some buildings about halfway.

At a T-junction, turn right and, after 150m, turn left onto a tree-lined bridleway. After 350m emerge into open fields, taking the left fork and following a bridleway (west) just inside a field with a boundary on the left. After 450m, the bridleway angles half right, cutting the field corner, towards a gap. Go through the gap and follow the same line towards a far coppice of mixed woodland. On reaching the woodland, don't pass through it, but instead fork left onto a track beside a wall on the right. After 1.2km at a wayside stone, the track bends slightly left. After a further 400m the route deviates slightly into and then out of **Ford Hill Farm** before resuming the same line (now on a metalled driveway) for another 600m to reach a road. Enjoy the fine Cotswold views of big skies and colourful rolling hills with the occasional farm or homestead.

Cross and enter the racehorse-training establishment of **Jackdaw's Castle**. Walk ahead on the sealed drive for 800m where signs direct you right, over the gallops. Cross cautiously to the far sealed drive, turn left and continue downhill for 1.1km to **Ford** and The Plough inn. Jackdaw's Castle, owned and run by Jonjo O'Neill, has trained winners of the Grand National and the Cheltenham Gold Cup.

Ford to Lynes Barn Farm — 3.4km, 1hr 5min

Having emerged from the footpath onto the **B4077**, turn right (west), passing a postbox and phone booth and crossing the infant **River Windrush**; take permissive paths in the left verge to reach the road left towards Temple Guiting. A few metres from the junction, take the footpath going up the hill (west), with a hedgerow on the left. At the hill crest, pass left through a gap, continuing, now with a low wall on the right and, beyond that, a quarry. The Cotswolds has many quarries, extracting the honey-coloured Oolitic Limestone, still prized for home building. Turn left when you reach a lane by **Slade Barn Farm**.

Follow this narrow, winding lane for 1.9km, passing the road signed to Farmcote. (Alternatively take the road to Farmcote, for tea and camping at Hayles Fruit Farm, where the Cotswold Way (Winchcombe Way) can be followed to Winchcombe, adding 1.5km or 25 minutes). Continue past the lane on the left by **Lynes Barn Farm**. The 'strip lynchets' marked on the map indicate the ancient terracing still visible on the hillside.

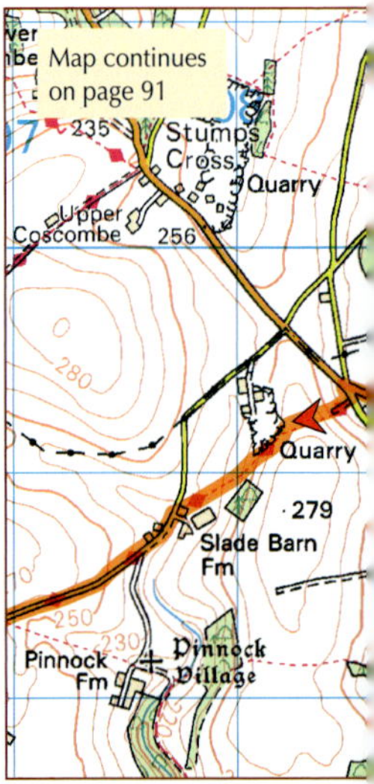

Lynes Barn Farm to Winchcombe — 4.8km, 1hr 15min

Just after the lane, leave the road through a gate on the right, then turn left to follow the track that contours round the hillside past a large old barn. Beyond this, pass

Little Farmcote

through a boundary and 100m further fork left into woodland through a steel gate. Shortly exit the woodland and continue to contour along the track towards Little Farmcote. After 700m pass through a gate, where angle right towards the corner of the fence going round the compound, and follow on the left to reach a kissing gate.

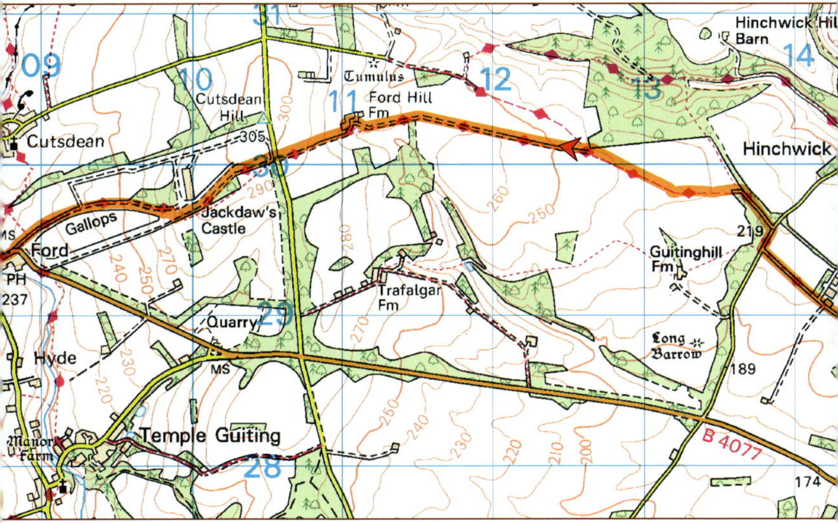

Enter the farmyard and then turn right and exit through the main gates. Take the leftmost track inclining slightly uphill to cross the old Salt Way (here a minor road) to a footpath. Contour across two fields to the gate on the skyline and turn left up to a stile into a small copse. There are fine views of the Cotswold Scarp, Gloucestershire Warwickshire Railway, Dumbleton Hill and beyond to Bredon Hill, with the flatlands of the Avon heading north.

SALT

From time immemorial salt has been a valuable commodity: a necessity for food-preservation and good health. Roman soldiers were paid in salt (Latin: *sal*, hence salary). If necessary, traders created routes, but more often would use existing ancient paths, as here, to transport the salt from source (Droitwich) to destination (Lechlade on Thames). Winchcombe Abbey owned salt rights in Droitwich as did other local manors and the routes used then have become the roads of today. We crossed previously at Salperton (the prefix *sal* is a giveaway) which possibly was an overnight stop for pack-horses and drivers.

Navigation ahead is tricky: keep an eye on your GPS. Exit the copse and descend through scrubby woodland to a kissing gate, where the slope gentles. Keep the field boundary on the right loosely nearby. Sight Langley Hill, ahead

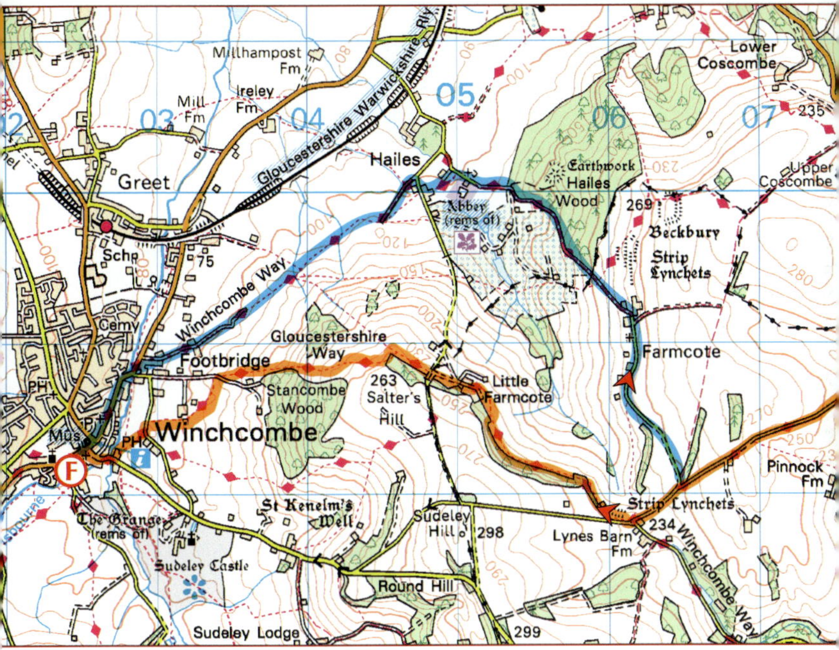
Millhampost Fm
Mill Fm
Ireley Fm
Gloucestershire Warwickshire Rly
Hailes
Lower Coscombe
Upper Coscombe
Greet
Earthwork
Hailes Wood
Abbey (rems of)
269
Beckbury
Strip Lynchets
Schs
75
Winchcombe Way
Cemy
Gloucestershire Way
Farmcote
Footbridge
263
Little Farmcote
Stancombe Wood
Salter's Hill
Winchcombe
PH
Mus
Pinnock Fm
St Kenelm's Well
Strip Lynchets
The Grange (rems of)
Sudeley Hill
298
Lynes Barn Fm
234
Winchcombe Way
Sudeley Castle
Round Hill
Sudeley Lodge
299
03
04
05
06
07
235

(west): this is our direction. Some 370m on from the kissing gate, take a wooden hand gate in the right fence, and turn half-left (still with Langley Hill ahead), towards a gap into trees. Here the path steepens again, becoming muddy under the trees. Eventually emerge from the woods and Winchcombe will be in view. As you descend, the field narrows and, ignoring a stony track heading left to a large aerial, find the kissing gate ahead equidistant from both field corners. Maintain the same line, crossing two small scrubby fields and exiting onto Stancombe Lane. Cross this slightly right and enter a large field.

The extremely large signs marking the path are unmissable. Walk across the field, erring slightly right, towards a gate (and a $1m^2$ sign) in the far boundary. Here, turn half-right, walking between a line of ancient oak trees to diagonally cross the field and exit just to the left of Stancombe Farm buildings. Turn half-right again, walk directly down the gentle slope and exit onto a lane. Turn left and after about 50m turn right into a field. Cross the field diagonally to the far corner and pass through a narrow passage between houses to the road. Turn right. Cross the **River Isbourne** (that flows into the Avon and thence the Severn) and walk up the short steep hill into **Winchcombe**.

WINCHCOMBE

Gargoyle on St Peter's Church, Winchcombe

Winchcombe is an attractive Cotswold town which retains a healthy mixture of shops and amenities. In the centre is a small museum relating Winchcombe's rich history. Kenelm, a grandson of the Mercian King Offa, was murdered here, and the town became a site of pilgrimage. This contributed wealth to the abbey, which was founded in 798 and dissolved by Henry VIII in the 16th century. The parish church of St Peter was paid for by abbey funds, and is worth visiting, with its grimacing gargoyles. A more recently arrived attraction fell from the heavens on 28 February 2021: the Winchcombe meteorite, which can also be seen in the museum.

STAGE 8

Winchcombe to Tewkesbury

Start	Winchcombe
Finish	Tewkesbury Abbey
Alternative routes	Dixton Hill to Woolstone Hill Farm; Claydon Farm to Walton Cardiff
Time	5hr 5min
Distance	18.2km (11.3 miles)
Ascent	265m
Descent	345m
Maps	OL45: The Cotswolds; Explorer 179: Gloucester, Cheltenham & Stroud; Explorer 190: Malvern Hills & Bredon Hill
Refreshments	None on route. The Shutters Inn, Gotherington (1km off route)
Public transport	Buses: a bus runs along the minor road between Winchcombe and Gotherington. Buses at Tewkesbury. Trains: at Ashchurch (1km from route, 4.5km from the route end); Gloucestershire Warwickshire Steam Railway (GWSR) runs nearby (see below)
Accommodation	Stanley Pontlarge; Prescott; Tewkesbury

This final stretch of the Gloucestershire Way links the small town of Winchcombe in the Cotswolds with the larger urban centre of Tewkesbury, and its magnificent abbey. The stage starts with a stiff climb out of Winchcombe and splendid panoramic views which open up over the town and northeastwards towards Broadway. The views only get better as you crest Langley Hill, bringing into sight Bredon Hill and finally the far-stretching Severn Vale, with the Malverns and Hay Bluff away to the west.

At Dixton, walkers can compare today's views with those from the 18th century, captured in the paintings at Dixton Manor.

From Oxenton the route winds through farmland and housing across flatlands to Tewkesbury. This is a flood plain, so in winter or after heavy rain the going can be wet – particularly the final few kilometres.

The end of the journey is at Tewkesbury Abbey, which is a jewel of English church architecture, and you should allow time for a leisurely visit.

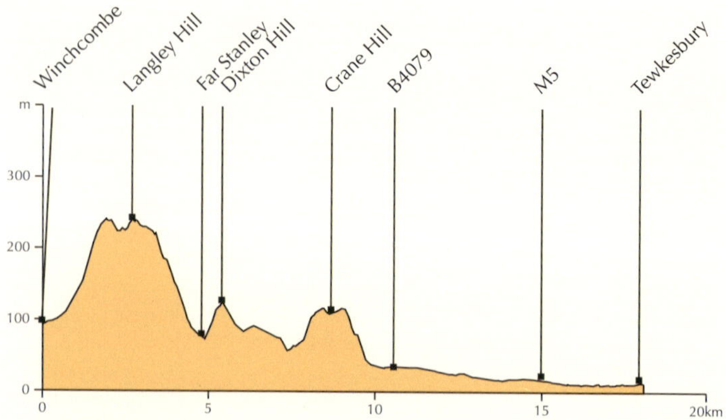

Winchcombe to Stanley

4.8km, 1hr 30min

Leave **Winchcombe** via Gloucester Street (**B4632**) passing St Peter's Church and its splendid gargoyles. At The Corner Cupboard Inn (currently closed), turn right into Malthouse Lane, then left into Langley Road, and first right into Harveys Lane. Walk 650m uphill and, having passed Enfield Farm, take the footpath

Winchcombe from Langley Hill

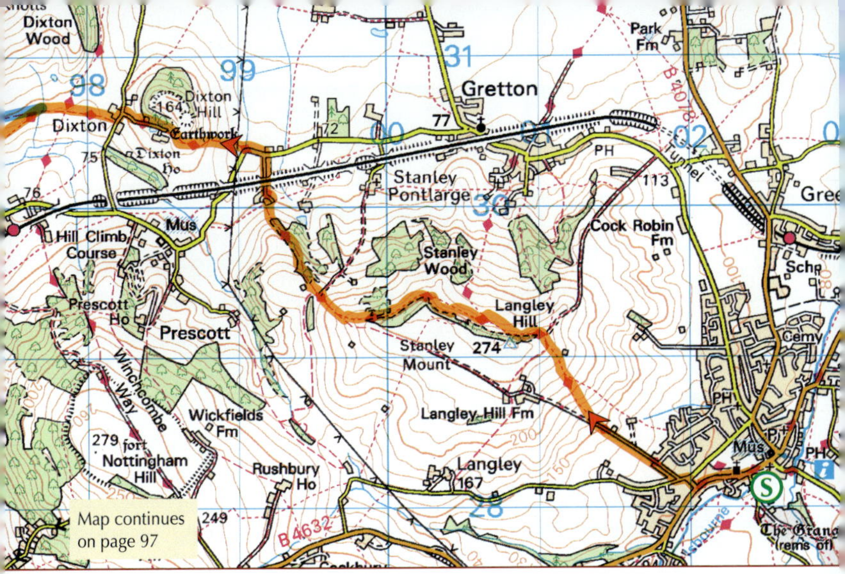

Map continues on page 97

through a kissing gate on the right. Cross the field diagonally, going steeply uphill towards the far corner. Maintain this line through a series of fields to reach a track at the top. Turn right and at a junction, Abbots Leys, go through the right-hand gate, turn left, walk 20m, and turn left through a kissing gate back onto the track. Now continue on the track west, contouring the hillside. There are fine views from here. GWSR trains are easier to hear than see.

Contour for 500m, staying close to the woodlands on the left. Walk past the ruins of an old farm, then through a field gate and continue for another 350m where you need to find the wooden hand gate at the top left corner of the field. The path bears left, still contouring. After 600m a bridleway joins from the left, then turns right and descends to a small plateau. Cross the plateau to the right of a ruined barn and shortly turn right into a holloway which you then follow for 350m down to the hamlet of Far Stanley. Turn right and follow the lane under the railway to the road.

The **Gloucestershire Warwickshire Steam Railway** (GWSR) is a volunteer-operated heritage railway, hauling steam and diesel trains between Cheltenham Racecourse and Broadway. Trains run throughout the year, although the service varies seasonally. The nearest stations to the Gloucestershire Way are Gotherington Halt (1km off route) and Winchcombe Station (1.6km off route).

Gloucestershire Warwickshire Steam Railway locomotive

Stanley to Oxenton Church **4.9km, 1hr 25min**

Turn left and walk (with care) to the bend, where you continue through the bridle gate and pass over the shoulder of **Dixton Hill** and descend past the manor, to a small road. Turn left, walk 70m, then turn right onto a bridleway and cross two fields.

THE DIXTON MANOR PAINTINGS

The Dixton Manor paintings, now hanging in The Wilson Cheltenham Art Gallery & Museum, were commissioned by past owners of Dixton Manor, and date from around 1715. Both are notionally from a viewpoint at the top of Dixton Hill, one looking southwest over Dixton Manor House towards Gotherington, the other looking east over fields towards Gretton. The pictures have a Brueghelesque quality, showing details of the Higford family, then owners of the manor, and of the work of bringing in the harvest. The gallery is worth a visit to view the paintings, which also include an early depiction of Morris dancing. The artist (as yet unknown) painted with some licence, but it is possible to roughly frame the same views now, although these are somewhat occluded by woodland and scrub. More information is available on the museum's website: wilsonmuseum.org.uk.

Main route

We recommend that you stray here from the main OS-marked Gloucestershire Way. This main route contours slightly left, rounding the hillside and passing through this and three further fields (more-or-less following the wires, above). In the last field, turn half-left and aim downhill at the edge of a marshalling yard with abandoned vehicles, where you turn right and pass through **Woolstone Hill** farmyard. This route is regularly ploughed or cropped.

Alternative route

The better option is to continue with the ascending bridleway ahead. Pass over two fields and pick up a green verge at the top alongside the left-hand boundary. Reaching a stony track, descend left to **Woolstone Hill** farmhouse, where you bear right at a large barn and exit onto the metalled driveway where the OS-marked route is rejoined. (Gotherington is about 1.5km south.)

Main route

Walk (west) about 250m along the lane to a footpath on the right after **Crane Hill Farm**. Climb steeply, initially close to a hedge, but as the slope gentles, bear right over the shoulder of the hill to a stile.

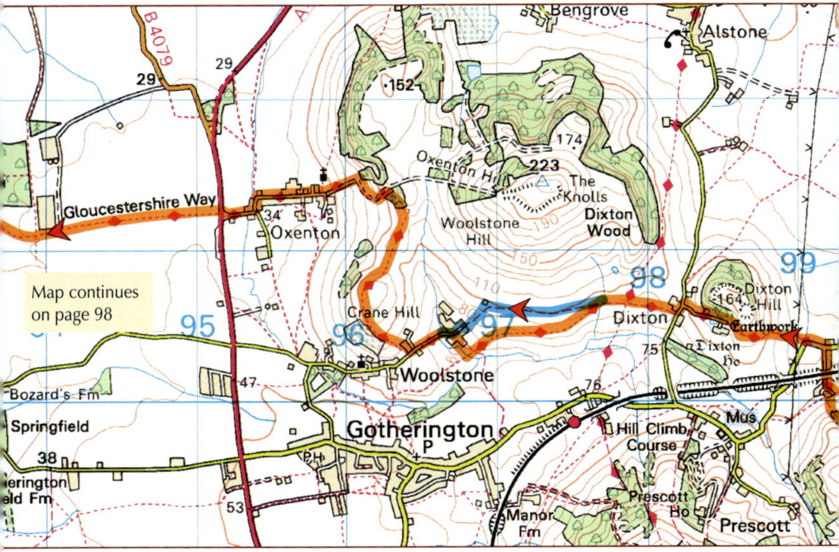

Map continues on page 98

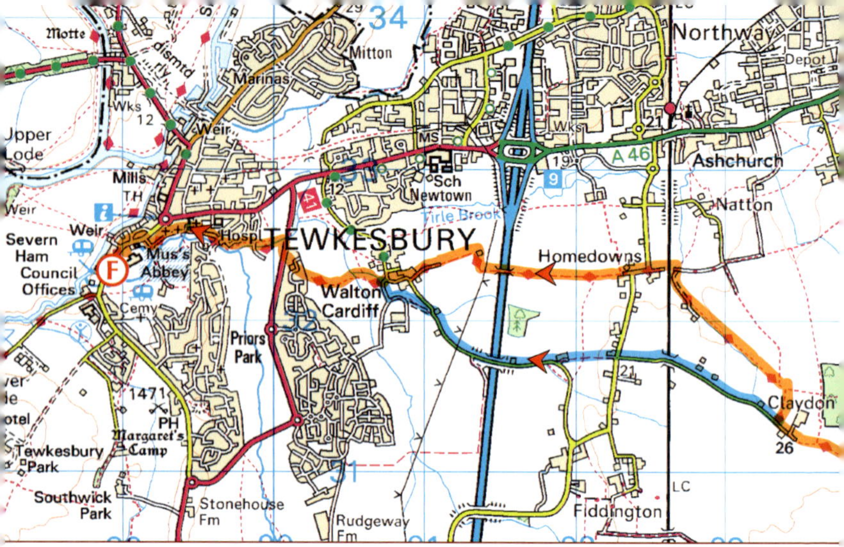

Clockwise, from the east, the views from **Crane Hill** take in Dixton Hill, Langley Hill, Nottingham Hill, Cotswold Scarp heading south, Cheltenham with Christ Church and the Racecourse prominent, Robinswood Hill, Churchdown Hill, Gloucester Cathedral, Severn Bridges, Forest of Dean, May Hill, Sugar Loaf, Hay Bluff, Tewkesbury Abbey, the Malvern Hills and Bredon Hill.

Cross the next field converging with a fence on the left, by pollarded ash trees. Continue next to the fence, reaching a coppice. Pass through this and at the exit turn left to join a 4WD track curving downhill. Where the track runs out, turn left to a gate with the church below. Descend into **Oxenton**. The church of St John the Baptist has 13th-century elements and interesting frescos.

Oxenton Church to Ashchurch Road — 4.5km, 1hr 10min

Go ahead, through the village, for 800m to the **A435** Cheltenham to Evesham road. Cross slightly right to the footpath heading along a stony track. After 750m, at a field boundary, the right hedge ends but you should continue in the same direction, to a stile in the hedge about 50m left of farm buildings. Cross the small scrubby field to a gate onto a green lane. Cross left to a stile, and continue, remaining about 15m from the ditch on the left. Pass through the gate onto an enclosed track and on to the small road by **Claydon Farm**. Walk about 100m along the road to a bridge and kissing gate on the right.

Alternative route

The main route involves a railway crossing. There may be some future temporary closures. Please check the Cicerone website for updates. An alternative route (about the same distance and time) is to continue along the road here for 1.3km to reach a bridleway ahead, which takes you to another lane, where you continue for a further 1.2km to reach **Walton Cardiff**.

Main route

For the main route, walk through the kissing gate and follow the right-hand hedge to a cross hedge where you turn left for 20m. Cross the field diagonally right to a footbridge (just to the left of the far corner of the field, orientate towards the Malverns' second peak from the right) over Tirle Brook.

Turn right along the hedge and, from the corner, continue on the same line to a stile in the distant hedge and there keep on. Alternatively, turn left after the bridge and follow the field boundary, which U-turns to continue north-west, through boundaries, eventually reaching the driveway.

Converge with the hedge on the left to join a surfaced driveway. Follow this right for 180m to a T-junction where turn left (or take the footpath straight ahead for Ashchurch Station) and cross the railway with extreme care.

Ashchurch Road to Tewkesbury Abbey — **4km, 1hr**

Pass a business park and, when you reach the busy Ashchurch Road, continue straight on for 100m and then bear off onto a bridleway. Follow this, jinking left

Tewkesbury Abbey

then right by The **Homedowns**, and continuing for 900m, passing over housing estate access roads, then cross the M5 via a footbridge.

Go through two old gateways, turn right, and follow the field edge for 150m to a small pond with willows. Turn left to continue following the right boundary. After 350m, enter an enclosed track which leads past homesteads to a minor road at **Walton Cardiff**. The alternative route (above) rejoins here.

At the road turn right, walk round a sharp bend to a junction, where you take the left fork which curves left round a pond. After 40m, at the apex of the bend, take the footpath on the right which follows the line of a brook on the right. Another 100m further on there is a meeting of footpaths, but stay with the brook on your right, angling slightly left to a bridge over a water course (which often floods the path). Cross the bridge and follow the hedge on the right for 110m to a gap. Go through the gap and cross the next wide field diagonally towards the far-left corner. Walk around the corner to spot a hand gate ahead which gives onto a surfaced path leading past houses before slanting right down to a cycleway.

Turn right, passing beneath the **A38** and onto a hard path, with **Tirle Brook** on the right. On reaching a cross track, turn right over the red-brick footbridge, then immediately left, following the brook, now on your left. When the path reaches Link Road, cross over, and pass through the children's playground to the road beyond, which you follow to **Tewkesbury Abbey**.

TEWKESBURY

Tewkesbury is a bustling medieval town at the confluence of the Severn and Avon rivers. Its strategic importance has lasted for centuries, in spite of periodic flooding, when only the Abbey stands proud of the waters. This is one of England's most splendid churches, described by Simon Jenkins as part of the great 'legacy left by monastic Catholicism to parochial Anglicanism after the Reformation'. The Abbey still contrives to have its own bishop.

Various other medieval buildings cluster around the Abbey, including The John Moore Museum, housed in a 15th-century timber-framed building, and The Merchant's House, which is a restored Tudor shop and home.

Both the Severn and Avon rivers are navigable at Tewkesbury, which has its own marina. For those with time and stamina, the Severn Way passes here, en route to the river's source, high in the Cambrian Mountains, in Wales.

In July each year the town is decorated with flags and pageantry as part of the free Medieval Festival which celebrates the Battle of Tewkesbury, fought on 4 May 1471. The battle, which was decisive in the Wars of the Roses, is re-enacted and the town is given over to Medieval enthusiasts. More information is available at: visittewkesbury.info.

APPENDIX A

Accommodation

Listings are within 2km of the route unless otherwise indicated. All require booking beforehand. Listings for larger towns are not provided, but visitor websites are included in Appendix B. Holiday lets are not included, as these are rarely available for one-night stays. There is limited camping en route. However, sites other than those listed may pop up or may be found on various dedicated websites. Wild camping is not permitted anywhere on the route.

hotel · B&B/guesthouse · self catering · hostel · camping

Stage/Location	Name	Type	Post code	Telephone	Web/email	Comments
Stage: 1 Chepstow to Parkend						
Chepstow						
St Briavels	YHA	hostel	GL15 6RG	+44 345 371 9042	yha.org.uk/hostel/yha-st-briavels-castle	4km off route
Parkend	The Fountain Inn	hotel	GL15 4JD	+44 1594 562189	thefountaininn.info	
	Whitemead Forest Park	self catering, camping	GL15 4LA	+44 3301 230374	whitemead.co.uk	Glamping options also available
	Deanfield B&B	B&B/guesthouse	GL15 4JF	+44 7968 603107	deanfield.co	
Stage 2: Parkend to Boxbush						
Coleford	The Speech House Hotel	hotel	GL16 7EL	+44 1594 822607	thespeechhouse.co.uk	
Longhope	The Yew Tree	hotel	GL17 0QD	+44 1452 830355	theyewtreeatlonghope.com	
Drybrook, Mitcheldean	Greenway Farm	camping	GL17 9HW	+44 7880 700513	greenwayfarm.org	3km off route
Upper Boxbush	Farmers Boy Inn	hotel	GL17 0LP	+44 1452 470109	farmersboyinn.co.uk	

Stage/Location	Name	Type	Post code	Telephone	Web/email	Comments
Stage 3: Boxbush to Gloucester						
May Hill	Glasshouse Inn		GL17 0NN	+44 7774 460711	quality-inns.co.uk/pubs/the-glasshouse-inn	Pub with three lodges
Huntley	The Red Lion Inn		GL19 3DU	+44 1452 913297	theredlioninnhuntley@gmail.com	
	The Kings Head, Birdwood		GL19 3EF	+44 1452 750348	No website	Book via online booking sites
Minsterworth	Naight House Bed and Breakfast		GL2 8JJ	+44 1452 751045	naighthouse.co.uk	
	Broadway Farm Camping		GL2 8JZ	+44 7852 356418	broadwayfarmcamping.com	2.4km off route
Over	The Lock Keepers		GL2 8DB	+44 1452 332900	thelockkeepers.co.uk	
Gloucester						
	Court Farm Camping		GL2 9PX	+44 1452 730326	gloucestercamping.co.uk	
Stage 4: Gloucester to Shurdington						
Twigworth	The Oakwood Hotel		GL2 9PG	+44 1452 905452	oakwoodhotel.co.uk	
Down Hatherley	Frog Furlong Cottage Country Guest House		GL2 9QE	+44 1452 730430	frogfurlong.co.uk	
	Hatherley Manor		GL2 9QA	+44 1452 730217	hatherleymanor.com	3km off route
Churchdown	The Old Elm Inn		GL3 2ER	+44 1452 530961	theoldelminn.co.uk	3km off route

Stage/Location	Name	Type	Post code	Telephone	Web/email	Comments
Shurdington	Stable Lodge B&B		GL51 4TY	+44 1242 431859	thestablelodge.co.uk	
	The Greenway Hotel and Spa		GL51 4UG	+44 1242 862352	thegreenwayhotelandspa.com	
Cheltenham						Off route
Stage 5: Shurdington to Shipton Oliffe						
Ullenwood/ Crickley Hill	Star Glamping		GL53 9QU	+44 1242 527631	nationalstar.org/visit-us/starglamping	2km off route
Birdlip	Royal George Hotel		GL4 8JH	+44 1452 862506	greenekinginns.co.uk/hotels/gloucestershire/royal-george-hotel	2.5km off route
Cowley	The Cowley Manor Hotel		GL53 9NL	+44 1242 870900	cowleymanorexperimental.com	1.5km off route
Cockleford	The Green Dragon Inn		GL53 9NW	+44 1242 870 271	green-dragon-inn.co.uk	2.4km off route
Upper Coberley	Big Skies Camping and Glamping		GL53 9RE	+44 7866 672831	bigskiesglamping.co.uk	2.5km off route
Shipton Oliffe	The Frogmill		GL54 4HT	+44 1242 386364	thefrogmill.co.uk	
Stage 6: Shipton Oliffe to Stow-on-the-Wold						
Cold Aston	The Plough Inn		GL54 3BN	+44 1451 822602	coldastonplough.com	
Lower Slaughter	The Slaughters Inn		GL54 2HS	+44 1451 822143	theslaughtersinn.co.uk	
	The Slaughters Manor House		GL54 2HP	+44 1451 820456	slaughtersmanor.co.uk	

Stage/Location	Name	Type	Post code	Telephone	Web/email	Comments
Bourton-on-the-Water						2 km off route Tourist honey pot, but with numerous hotel/B&B options
	The Wildings Campsite		GL54 2LF	+44 1451 518869	thewildingscampsite.co.uk	3.8km off route
	Field Barn Park Camping		GL54 2LF	+44 1451 821260	fieldbarnpark.com	Adults only campsite
Stow-on-the-Wold						Hotel/B&B options; sadly, the youth hostel is now closed
Stage 7: Stow-on-the-Wold to Winchcombe						
Upper Swell	Woodland Guest House		GL54 1EW	+44 1451 832346	woodland-guesthouse.igloucestershire.com	
Winchcombe						
	Hayles Fruit Farm		GL54 5PB	01242 602123	haylesfruitfarm.co.uk/campsite	2.7km off route
Stage 8: Winchcombe to Tewkesbury						
Stanley Pontlarge	Middle Stanley		GL54 5HE	+44 1242 673119	middlestanley.co.uk	Single-night stays are not always possible
Prescott	Pardon Hill Farm		GL52 9RD	+44 1242 677406	pardonhillfarm.co.uk	
Tewkesbury						
	Lower Lode Inn		GL19 4RE	+44 7813 883605	lowerlodeinn.co.uk/camp	1.5km from route end

APPENDIX B

Useful information

Public transport

Public transport in the area is regular, but infrequent. Plan your journey before setting off each day and, where possible, travel by public transport at the start of the day rather than the end (easier to schedule, often additional services for schools, and you don't need to stress about the speed you are walking). Make sure you have the Traveline App on your phone, and possibly others too.

Buses

Listed roughly according to when met on the route.

Newport Bus Company
newportbus.co.uk
72 Chepstow–Lydney–Cinderford–Mitcheldean

FR Willetts
willettscoaches.co.uk
7 Cinderford–Speech House–Parkend–Lydney (limited service)

Stagecoach
stagecoachbus.com
23 Coleford–Bream–Lydney–A48–Gloucester
22 Lydney–Coleford–Cinderford–Westbury–A48–Gloucester
24 Coleford–Speech House–Cinderford-–Mitcheldean–Huntley–A40–Gloucester (starts/terminates at Cinderford after 1605)
33 Ross-on-Wye–Mitcheldean–Longhope–Huntley–A40–Gloucester
71 Tewkesbury–A38–Twigworth–Longford–Gloucester
94, 95, 96
Gloucester–Brickhampton–B4063–Cheltenham
97, 98 Gloucester–Churchdown–Cheltenham
10 Gloucester–A46–Shurdington–Cheltenham
66 Stroud–Gloucester Business Park–A46–Shurdington–Cheltenham
882 Cirencester–Birdlip–Gloucester (school-time service only)
51 Cheltenham–A435–Coberley–Cirencester
W Winchcombe–Cheltenham
41, 42, 43, 43A
Tewkesbury–Cheltenham

Pulhams
pulhams.co.uk
801 Chipping Norton–Morton–Stow-on-the-Wold–Bourton-on-the-Water–A436–Shipton–Cheltenham
606 Chipping–Campden–Winchcombe–Gotherington–Bishop's Cleeve–Cheltenham

Trains

See nationalrail.co.uk. There are stations at Chepstow, Lydney, Gloucester, Cheltenham, Ashchurch (for Tewkesbury). A station at Moreton-in-Marsh is on the Oxford–Worcester Parkway line.

Heritage Railways
Gloucestershire Warwickshire Steam Railway
gwsr.com
Broadway–Cheltenham Racecourse. Halts at Winchcombe and Gotherington. Cheltenham Racecourse is some distance from the mainline station.

Dean Forest Railway
deanforestrailway.co.uk
Lydney–Parkend

Information points

Chepstow Castle Car Park
Bridge St
Chepstow
NP16 5EY
tel +44 1291 623772

Stow Tourist Information
St Edwards Hall
Stow-on-the-Wold
GL54 1AG

Visitor websites

Chepstow
visitmonmouthshire.com/explore/chepstow

Forest of Dean
visitdeanwye.co.uk

Coleford
colefordtown.net

Gloucester
visitgloucester.co.uk

Cheltenham
visitcheltenham.com

Cotswolds
cotswolds.com
cotswolds.org
visitcotswolds.co.uk

Bourton-on-the-Water
bourtoninfo.com

Winchcombe
winchcombe.co.uk

Tewkesbury
visittewkesbury.co.uk

Useful websites

Gloucestershire County Council – Public Rights of Way (please report problems!)
gloucestershire.gov.uk/prow

Cotswold National Landscape
cotswolds-nl.org.uk

Forestry England
forestryengland.uk/the-forest-of-dean

A417 works progress and information
nationalhighways.co.uk/our-roads/south-west/a417-missing-link

Gloucester Cathedral
gloucestercathedral.org.uk

Tewkesbury Abbey
tewkesburyabbey.org.uk

Further information

The Dixton Manor paintings
wilsonmuseum.org.uk/collection/the-dixton-manor-paintings

Gloucestershire Geology
glosgeotrust.org.uk/index.shtml

All things tick-related
gov.uk/government/collections/ticks

Useful services and apps

This book is available in the Cicerone app on your phone. View GPS-enabled maps you can download for offline navigation, check route details and local points of interest, and plan your adventure with confidence. GPX files are also available to download. See cicerone.co.uk/1294.

Transport: Stagecoach, Pulhams, National Rail, Traveline

Weather: eg BBC Weather or Met Office

A road-mapping app: eg Google Maps or Apple Maps (although these are not sufficient for off-road navigation)

Text 999: Everyone should register for this service. It takes about 10 seconds to do. Handy in multiple situations. Search "Text 999" to find out more.

Baggage transfer companies

Currently, there are no companies specifically operating along the Gloucestershire Way, so expect to carry your bags or make your own arrangements. But there are companies working along other nearby routes that may offer you a day or two's respite.

Carryabag
carryabag.co.uk
Covers the Cotswold Way

Luggage Transfers
luggage-transfers.co.uk
Covers the Cotswold Way

Walk Lite
walklitebt.co.uk
Covers the Wye Valley Walk and Offa's Dyke Path in their southern sections (ie starting in Chepstow)

CICERONE

Hello, and thank you for choosing a Cicerone guide!

It takes the combined dedication of many to create the book you now hold. Our authors explore the world to find the best routes; they research, write, record data and take stunning photos on the trail to inspire and guide new adventures. Then, our talented team work together with authors to create the best products for our readers, whether digital or printed. The final part of the picture is you; we deeply value hearing from Cicerone customers with ideas and updates from the trail. Your input helps us to improve and innovate across our guides.

Cicerone is proud to be a family business. Exploring the outdoors has always been central to our lives, and we are passionate about sharing our love of walking, trekking, cycling and climbing. If you have any feedback or just want to say hello, please get in touch – we would love to hear from you.

Happy adventuring,
Joe & Maddy

Contact us at

hello@cicerone.co.uk **cicerone.co.uk/contact**

The Cicerone story

1969 Cicerone is founded by Walt and Dorothy Unsworth and Brian and Aileen Evans, publishing Lakeland guides printed on a garage press.

1977 The *Tour of Mont Blanc* guidebook defines the modern trekking guide and establishes Cicerone internationally.

1999 Jonathan and Lesley Williams take over, bringing a deep love of the outdoors.

2011 Cicerone produces its first eBook.

2022 Joe and Maddy Williams take the helm, keeping Cicerone independent, family run and rooted in real adventure.

2026 The Cicerone App launches, bringing decades of trusted route knowledge, GPS-enabled maps and planning tools directly to your phone.

Discover more at **cicerone.co.uk/about-cicerone**